Punch & Judy

PUNCH & JUDY

THE DOUBLE DISILLUSION ELECTION OF 2010

Mungo MacCallum

Black Inc.

Published by Black Inc.,
an imprint of Schwartz Media Pty Ltd
37–39 Langridge Street
Collingwood Vic 3066 Australia
email: enquiries@blackincbooks.com
http://www.blackincbooks.com

The National Library of Australia Cataloguing-in-Publication entry:

MacCallum, Mungo (Mungo Wentworth), 1941-

Punch & Judy : the double disillusion election of 2010 /
Mungo MacCallum.

ISBN: 9781863955119 (pbk.)

Australia. Parliament--Elections--2010.
Australian Labor Party--History--2007-
Liberal Party of Australia--History--2007-
Australia--Politics and government--2007-

324.994

Book design by Thomas Deverall
Typeset by Duncan Blachford

Printed in Australia by Griffin Press

To Graham Freudenberg,
in memory of the great days when politics
was important, passionate and fun

Punch and Judy /*noun*. deception; an unbelievable story.
—ERIC PARTRIDGE, *A Dictionary of Slang and Unconventional English*

★ *Foreword*

THURSDAY 24 JUNE 2010 was a red-letter day for Australia, and we're not just talking about hair. Indeed, Julia Eileen Gillard may not even be the country's first ranga prime minister; since all the old ones appear only in black and white, we can't tell. But she is certainly our first female: well into the twenty-first century, Australia finally caught up with more advanced nations such as Turkey, Israel, the Philippines, Sri Lanka and Pakistan and installed a woman as its head of government.

Note the word 'installed': Gillard was not popularly elected but had greatness thrust upon her by party bosses who saw their government in danger of going down the gurgler. This was in the great Australian tradition that saw Carmen Lawrence burned in Western Australia and Joan Kirner sacrificed in Victoria; and it confirms the pattern that countries whose culture is basically misogynist are more likely to put what they see as the weaker sex into a leadership role than those where equality is more usually the norm. There have been exceptions, of course, but Australia is not one of them. So from the start, history suggested that Gillard was more likely to join the list of heroic failures – even political martyrs – than become the desired saviour. She would be in good company: the Amazon queen Hippolyta, the Pharaoh Hatshepsut, Boadicea and Joan of Arc come to mind.

But Gillard had other things in mind. In her own assessment, and in that of her supporters, she was born to be prime minister; she had no interest in assuming the role of a gallant loser. She claimed to take as her political model Bob Hawke, who won four elections – a Labor record. But she must also have considered the example of his replacement, Paul Keating. Like Keating, Gillard had been given the job by a party that feared defeat under its previous leadership. Keating had not been expected to win the election that followed; the idea was that he would minimise the loss and save enough furniture in 1993 to set Labor up for next time. But he went on to win the unwinnable election and earn himself a place in Labor's pantheon.

On the surface Gillard's task appeared easier. The polls still favoured the government, and the election was approaching fast; Gillard could expect at least a brief honeymoon with the voters and should be able to sail home before it ended. And more importantly the Opposition, after two leadership changes, remained pretty shambolic; its current leader, Tony Abbott, appeared far less popular or electable than had John Hewson seventeen years earlier. Gillard also felt that she was ready for the job: she had been an effective and loyal deputy for nearly three years, acting in the top job for 185 days on twenty-seven separate occasions, and she was determined not to get caught like Keating, whose chance came too late for his real ambition, or worse still like Peter Costello, whose chance never came at all. She had lived through the highs and lows of the Kevin Rudd rollercoaster and believed she knew where he went wrong. And she had plenty of people to warn her if she began making the same mistakes.

After all, over that rough political ride she had been the woman closest to Rudd – except, of course, for Thérèse Rein the wife and Abby the dog. But it's fair to say that six months earlier, none of them suspected the fate that awaited them on the feast of the nativity of John the Baptist. Indeed, at the start of 2010, things must have looked altogether bright for the extended Rudd family as they shuffled comfortably between the Lodge in Canberra and Kirribilli House in Sydney, making the most of the Indian summer. At least, we hope they made the most of it. The winter would prove pretty bleak.

> ❝ *I can laugh at a puppet show, at the same time I*
> *know there is nothing in it worth my attention*
> *or regard.* —LADY MARY WORTLEY MONTAGU

★ 1.

JASPER THE CAT AND ABBY THE DOG thought that 2010 was going to be a good year. They had settled nicely into their spacious new surroundings at the Lodge and were about to be immortalised in print. Malcolm Turnbull's dogs, Mellie and Jo Jo, might have had their own blog, but Jasper and Abby were going into Allen & Unwin hardback, a far more prestigious apotheosis.

The book had been a closely guarded secret, which made its release in January all the more exciting. It turned out to be a well-publicised triumph, with rave reviews and, it must be admitted, not a few attempts at parody; but hey, imitation is the sincerest form of flattery. And now, a wonderful follow-up: Abby collected the *Weekend Australian* on 23 January to find that her human, the statesman, scholar and author Kevin Michael Rudd, had been named Australian of the Year.

Well, not the official Australian of the Year – that title had gone to an obscure Melbourne psychiatrist. But in its own way this award was even more unexpected. Kevin was Rupert Murdoch's very own Australian of the Year. Just as the Sun King hands out his own journalism awards to his own journalists, so he promotes his own nobility, and this year the lucky winner was Kevin Rudd. Clearly the judging panel had not included such Murdoch luminaries as Andrew Bolt, Piers Akerman, Dennis Shanahan and Janet Albrechtsen, as the front-page announcement was followed by several thousand words of lavish, indeed fulsome praise for Rudd's valour, resolution and economic success. Later in the same paper Christopher Pearson was allowed to pour the usual bucket of shit on him, but on balance it had to be counted as a big plus.

Unfortunately, closer examination revealed that the same award had been bestowed on every Australian prime minister since Billy McMahon; it went with the office. Indeed, if Rudd had missed out, it would have been a severe kick in the guts. But such considerations were not sufficient to cast a pall over the general rejoicing. Jasper and Abby were particularly chuffed. Now this really was a Great Australia Day Kerfuffle worth writing about.

It was particularly gratifying to start 2010 on a cheerful note, because 2009 had turned out to be something of an anti-climax. It had started with two huge challenges: the global financial crisis and climate change. Rudd had promoted both as almost apocalyptic threats at the start of his second year in office, and had made Churchillian speeches threatening the populace with blood and toil, tears and sweat as drastic measures were taken to tackle them.

But in the event, government action was mainly benign. The GFC was attacked by throwing money at it, and since a large portion of the dosh went through the bank accounts of Rudd's beloved working families, few of them objected. There was some pain, of course: unemployment went up, but by far less than the pundits had predicted. In the end, Australia emerged in far better shape than anyone had dared hope and well ahead of the rest of the industrialised world. It was a relief and a victory, but there was also a vague sense that the encroaching catastrophe had been oversold in the first place.

The story of climate change was much the same. Again, Rudd's solution seemed designed to ensure that no one actually suffered, even the most damaging polluters. His emissions trading scheme (ETS) was seen by many of the experts as a cop-out, a way of ducking the hard decisions. Nor could he get it through parliament. And as in Australia, so in the rest of the world: the international gathering called to deliver cooperation and consensus dissolved into a morass of bickering that resolved exactly nothing. Overall, 2009 seemed to produce a lot of sound and fury, but not much else. Apocalypse not. Copenhagen phut.

So the lead-up to election year had not gone quite as Kevin Rudd, PM, had planned. And this was not only unexpected, it was very, very unfair. Rudd had, after all, just got Australia through the greatest financial crisis since the Great Depression. But quite suddenly the times were out of joint. Caught off balance, he had badly stuffed up over the issue of asylum seekers. And worst of all the Opposition, that bunch of complaisant patsies, had suddenly gone feral. It wasn't meant to be like this.

It would have been an exaggeration to describe his first two years in office as an unbroken series of triumphs; it could hardly be denied that there had been the odd hiccup. But Rudd could have been forgiven for thinking that these were completely overshadowed by the wins. Concerning the global financial crisis, there was daylight between us and the rest of the industrialised world, the big stimulus program had bloody well worked and the Opposition's mutterings about doing more with less could and should be dismissed as mere whingeing and carping.

And overseas he had really starred. The new super-charged G20, the vehicle which was going show to the way to a new, more efficient and more democratic world order, was at least partly his creation. Copenhagen had been a let-down, but everyone – well, nearly everyone – blamed the Chinese for that. The main thing was that Australia, or at least he, was back on the world stage. Bilaterally things weren't quite as flash; Indonesia was miffed about the boat people, India was touchy about its students, Japan was wailing about whaling and even China seemed to be getting uncooperative on a number of issues. But Rudd couldn't be blamed for that, or for anything else, really.

True, Fuel Watch and Grocery Watch hadn't really worked, but a lot of people had thought they were good ideas at the time. Okay, the education revolution was still in its formative stages, but an awful lot of buildings had gone up, even if they weren't always received with the gratitude they deserved. There had obviously been the odd bit of inefficiency and even rorting, but you can't make an omelet without chopping up a few *fines herbes*. Which reminded him: WorkChoices was well and truly chopped up. Perhaps not quite as finely as the unions would have liked, but a lot of the employers were complaining too, and you can't say fairer than that.

The broadbanding of Australia was under way; well, not quite in the manner in which it had been planned, but there were a few holes in the ground, particularly in Tasmania. The Murray–Darling Basin was still a battleground, but some of the premiers, or at least those who were the premiers at the time, had signed something which said something ought to be done about it. And speaking of the blame game, the hospital system was definitely on the agenda for this year, assuming there were not more pressing priorities.

True, there had not been as much concrete achievement as some would have hoped, but in a way even that was a positive; it wasn't that anyone really objected to anything he'd done, it was just that they wished he'd done more of it. And of course he would, but there was no need to rush into it. And hey, we'd had a GFC, remember? That was where the real action was, and don't forget it.

And there was another reason for self-congratulation: he had kept his election promises. During 2007 all the spin doctors, pollsters, sociologists, astrologers, necromancers and other psephological experts insisted that he be a conservative, and that meant agreeing with John Howard quite a lot. So he had promised to keep most of Howard's policies, even the really, really bad ones, and he had kept his promise. Sometimes he had kept it even more than he had meant to, but that was the work of the Senate. The Senate had been very naughty and he wouldn't forget in a hurry. But things had been pretty much under control right up to the very end; that nice Malcolm Turnbull had been poised to deliver the emissions trading scheme he needed until that horrible Nick Minchin organised an act of monstrous treason not only against his own leader, but against the government of Australia, indeed against the nation itself, and suddenly Crazy Tony Abbott was to be his opponent for election year.

This obviously required a major change of strategy. The game plan had been to coast through a few gentlemanly rounds with Turnbull, or at worst with his old mate Joe Hockey, a campaign fought under Queensberry rules with no kicking, gouging or biting. But not now; Abbott had already signalled that he would fight hard and he would fight dirty – after all, he was on a hiding to nothing and he knew it. But it shouldn't change things all that much. Abbott had been in politics longer than

Rudd, but no one had ever taken him seriously. And they weren't about to start now – were they?

★

Anthony John Abbott had never made any secret of his ambition. From the time his mother announced that he would become either the prime minister or the pope, young Tony realised he was destined for greatness; the only question was whether it would be of the secular or sacred kind. For many years he tried to combine the two, and in a sense he still did: like Kevin Rudd, he made it clear that his religion played a large part in his political life, but unlike Rudd, he saw his politics in a quasi-religious context. He spoke of it as a vocation, even a calling.

His biographer, Michael Duffy, notes that Abbott's first important mentor was a priest, Father Emmet Costello, a teacher at the Jesuit St Ignatius College, Riverview. The second was a mystic turned political operative, Bartholomew Augustine Santamaria, whom Abbott once described as the greatest living Australian. And the third was John Howard, for whom politics was a religion in its own right. This personal trinity bequeathed Abbott a somewhat medievalist view of the world; even after fifteen years in parliament, he remained more interested in ideals than ideas; and his ideals were, of course, those of the conservative wing of the Vatican.

His Catholicism was always muscular and at times worldly, but it was also unremittingly authoritarian; there was no room for doubt in Abbott's version of the universe. But while his values were set in stone, his approach to politics could be thoroughly pragmatic, even opportunistic. He was an enthusiastic and effective debater, prepared to argue passionately for whatever cause the moment dictated.

I've had my own first-hand experience of Abbott's erratic approach. When he was a junior minister we appeared on the same platform in a television show called *Australia Talks*, compered by George Negus, a sort of predecessor to *Q&A*. It ran live-to-air, with a studio audience asking questions of the so-called expert panel. I was seated next to Abbott, and as one questioner launched into an attack on the government, I was astonished to hear the minister musing audibly:

'Hmm, this could be a tricky one. How should I handle it? Let's see, I could blame the states, or perhaps call it a beat-up by the left-wing media ...'

As the microphones were open, some of this may well have gone to air. It occurred to me that Abbott, a noted boxer, had perhaps fought too many rounds without a helmet.

I already knew him to be a touch erratic: a solicitor friend told me she had lived in a student share-house with Abbott when they were both studying law at Sydney University. He had, she claimed, a disconcerting habit of wandering around the place naked. Eventually they asked him to leave. These were the days before he entered St Patrick's Seminary, where he would also have to leave, overcome with uncontrollable lust. Then there was the matter of his supposed illegitimate son, a tragi-comic saga that ended with the discovery that the boy had in fact been fathered by someone else. None of this behaviour disqualified him from political leadership; after all, he was following the trail blazed by Bob Hawke, and it was not so long since his own party had been led by John Grey Gorton. But it was, to put it mildly, a somewhat unusual CV for a self-styled conservative, whose supposed appeal was to the traditionalists who yearned to regain the certainties of the past.

It was tempting to compare his unexpected and almost accidental elevation with the Labor Party's embrace of Mark

Latham six years earlier. Faced with a desperate situation, the party room had decided to kick high and chase and hope for a lucky bounce. In Labor's case it had ended in tears; was there any reason to think the Liberals' experiment would be any more successful?

But while Latham and Abbott had much in common in terms of temperament and ambition, there was one important difference. When Latham became leader, he had no administrative experience; indeed he had only spent a brief time as a shadow minister, having resigned from Kim Beazley's front bench in a fit of pique. Abbott, on the other hand, had served as a minister for almost nine years, spending seven of them in cabinet and three in the vital and sensitive portfolio of Health. He had been a key member of a long-standing and stable government, an acknowledged member of the leadership group and a close confidant of the prime minister. In fact, Howard had encouraged Abbott to see himself as a future leader, at one time setting him up as a putative rival to Peter Costello. Abbott had always acknowledged that Costello was ahead of him, but he had also let it be known that he would be ready for the top job when his time came. And it came rather sooner than he, or anyone else, had expected.

Like his mentor John Howard, Abbott was, when the crunch finally came, the last man standing. He was certainly not the popular choice, either for the electorate or for his colleagues; both groups would have preferred the jolly compromise of Joe Hockey, described by Howard as 'a great big bear of a man' when given the job of persuading the public to eat a shit sandwich called WorkChoices. Hockey did not want the leadership; like Abbott, he saw himself as a contender after the next election, not at this one. The Liberals urged him to stand simply because he was neither Malcolm Turnbull nor Tony Abbott (nor, incredibly, Kevin Andrews – a figure used by parents to frighten recalcitrant children into obedience – who had offered himself as an alternative to Turnbull).

According to the polls, the public would actually have preferred Turnbull to Abbott and even within the party room it was a damned close-run thing: the final ballot saw Abbott win by one vote, with one abstention and one Turnbull supporter absent. But the real target was not Turnbull: it was his support for an emissions trading scheme. Some breathless commentators described it as a 'battle for the soul of the Liberal Party,' which was, frankly, hogwash. The Liberal Party is a purely pragmatic body formed with a single purpose in mind: to oppose the Labor Party. Where it has policies of its own (the GST, WorkChoices), these are more often than not arrived at by looking at what Labor would do and then proposing the reverse.

Turnbull, a genuine liberal (as opposed to Liberal), was always an exception to this rule. He believed that a party of the centre-right could be both modern and progressive; this idea outraged the reactionaries in the party room and the branches, both of which rose in a well-orchestrated campaign of protest. The symbolic issue on which it focused was Turnbull's support for an ETS.

The ETS policy was originally proposed by John Howard himself, but since his departure it had been remorselessly white-anted by the combined forces of the sceptics, the deniers, the rent-seekers, the ignorant and the simply bloody-minded. In the party room they were led by the sinister minister, the senator conspirator Nick Minchin, an ageing right-wing war lord from South Australia.

Minchin not only denied the reality of man-made global warming; he was sceptical about the entire discipline of science. His instincts were at one with the cardinals who condemned

Galileo. Ironically, Minchin accused the Greens of trying to 'de-industrialise' the world, while himself rejecting as communistic voodoo the science that made industrialisation possible. And it was this throwback to the Dark Ages who took it upon himself to determine the leadership and direction of the Liberal Party in the twenty-first century.

Minchin realised that Abbott was heartily disliked by large numbers of voters, especially women; while the hardline conservatives might embrace him as one of their own, he would be unlikely to gain the middle ground needed to win an election. Hockey was a much more palatable alternative; but Hockey, while prepared to abandon his promise not to stand against Turnbull, was not prepared to surrender his principles altogether. He actually believed in climate change and thought that an emissions trading scheme would be a useful tool in fighting it. The most he would offer Minchin was a free vote in the party room on the subject. But for Minchin, throwing out the ETS was non-negotiable. It was a Yes–No question, and Hockey was trying to answer 'Maybe.' Hockey was eliminated, and Andrews was clearly unelectable. Which left Abbott.

But even with the right's undivided backing, Abbott could only manage a majority of one – perhaps not even that had everyone been present and willing to vote. Half the Liberal Party preferred Turnbull, with all his abrasiveness and divisiveness; it is tempting to believe that they recognised that Turnbull, while not the most charismatic of politicians, at least represented the future, while Abbott, for all his self-promoted people skills, was a step backwards into the past. And if they had any doubts, Abbott immediately removed them by announcing his new (well, actually not) front bench.

Resurrecting Kevin Andrews might have been dismissed as unfortunate but understandable: it was Andrews, after all, who had pulled the initial trigger against Turnbull and set the conditions for Abbott's ascension. But giving the party's resident bogeyman responsibility for families, housing and human services – areas which would normally require a certain quotient of human empathy, if not actual compassion – was surely taking papal solidarity too far. And then, blinking from a long and well-deserved interment in the political crypt, Bronwyn Bishop emerged beside him as shadow minister for seniors. 'Well,' said Abbott in justification, 'you can't deny that she is one.' And the laughter had hardly died down when Phillip Ruddock – missing believed dead – was named as shadow cabinet secretary.

Indeed it turned out to be a cabinet of shadows, even of ghosts. The only real surprise was that Wilson Tuckey missed out; being both senile and mad he seemed to have all the necessary qualifications. The Nationals' Barnaby Joyce, not yet senile but undeniably mad, was not only welcomed into the tent but given the wide-ranging and sensitive portfolio of finance. He promptly proved that he could piss just as effectively into the tent from inside as he had from outside by announcing that both Queensland and the United States were effectively bankrupt and that Chinese investment should be banned. At least he was undeniably alive.

Abbott explained that he was up for a fight and that he wanted a team of fighters, street-hardened brawlers who, like him, would not take a backward step. He was leader of the Opposition and, by golly, he was going to oppose; he wasn't going to pretend to be a government-in-exile. It was a rousing call to arms, but it overlooked one thing: in fewer than twelve months there would be an election, at which Abbott and his team would be offering themselves as the alternative government. Since no rational voter could contemplate the idea of

Bishop or Ruddock, or probably Andrews, as ministers in a newly formed government, they were presumably expected to oppose like mad for a few months and then gracefully return to the vault. But it was difficult to imagine them even in that limited role.

Coalition supporters had spent the last two years in what was happily described by one Labor observer as a healthy spirit of defeatism. Except when crazed by strong drink, no one seriously believed that they could win an election in 2010, and even Abbott admitted that victory was, well, unlikely. He would emerge from the year, he prophesied, either as a political hero or as political road kill, and there were certainly more pundits standing around with shovels and garbage bags than with laurel wreaths. However, he showed his readiness for the contest by being photographed in Speedos, before following the advice of the pundits and constructing a story to tell the Australian people. Well, actually it wasn't so much a story as a fairytale. Rudd's ETS, he proclaimed, was just a great big new tax on everything, and that was all that needed to be said. But it wasn't – it was clear that climate change was going to remain a very big political issue, perhaps even the defining issue of the election campaign. Abbott had already locked the Coalition into a rejection of the ETS in any shape or form; the Nationals needed no persuading, and the Liberals had confirmed this position with a convincing secret ballot. But Abbott still needed to take a stance on climate change and, this time, stick to it. The question was, which stance? He had plenty to choose from.

When Howard adopted an ETS as policy in 2007, Abbott was one of its most dedicated advocates. When Malcolm Turnbull urged its acceptance rather than fight an election over the issue, Abbott was in the frontline of his supporters, encouraging his more reluctant colleagues to follow their leader. Not long afterwards he declared the science of climate change to be crap, then rejected the very idea of an ETS out of hand. On becoming leader of his party he claimed some unspecified form of 'direct action' was a better way of solving the problem than a market-based ETS. Even his confessor must have felt a little confused as to where he really stood, if anywhere at all. Greg Hunt, who had been retained as spokesman for climate change and the environment despite being a true believer in the ETS, must have been absolutely discombobulated. Caught between Nick Minchin in charge of resources and energy on one side and Ian Macfarlane in charge of infrastructure and water on the other, he was now charged with finding a coherent policy to replace the ETS in less than six weeks.

As a strategist on climate change, Abbott made General Custer look like Alexander the Great. Turnbull, quick to return to the fray, labelled Abbott a weathervane, framing policy according to the prevailing political breeze. However, such pedantry did not deter Abbott's cheer squad, which dutifully fell into formation in the pages of the Murdoch press. Leading the troops was, of course, Dennis Shanahan, who described one of Abbott's forthcoming speeches to the faithful (a copy of which just happened to have been leaked to him) as positively Churchillian; his wife, Angela, upped the ante by comparing Abbott to the first Christian martyr, St Stephen (you know, the one who got stoned). And Howard's old guru, Arthur Sinodinos (now running with Rupert's hyenas), suggested a still better analogy was with Spartacus, who led the slaves' revolt in ancient Rome; he did not point out that the revolt ended with Spartacus and all his followers being crucified beside the Appian Way.

It was left to the *Australian*'s dominatrix, Janet Albrechtsen, to bring the adulation back to earth: the real secret of Abbott's appeal, she asserted, was that he was wonderfully hairy. And indeed he was; we had the photos to prove it. The idea was that while dried-up old feminists might find Abbott a turn-off because of his dogmatic Catholicism – err, enlightened social conservatism – real women would vote for him because he was a real man: a boxer, a cyclist, a lifesaver, a volunteer fire-fighter, a far cry from the creepy metrosexual Kevin Rudd. Well, it was a theory, but unfortunately the polls failed to bear it out.

★

Abbott's first electoral test was with the by-elections for the seats vacated by his colleagues Brendan Nelson and Peter Costello. Since both were ultra-safe Liberal blue-ribbon electorates, Labor did not waste money by standing a candidate in either. This opened the door to the minor parties in Nelson's Sydney seat of Bradfield and a heavenly host of nine Christian Democrat candidates thrust themselves forward. But the real challenge, it was felt, would come from the Greens; in Costello's Melbourne seat of Higgins they put forward the high-profile activist Clive Hamilton. No one seriously expected the Liberals to lose either contest, but there was a hope among the more optimistic lefties that they might be driven to preferences.

In fact they weren't; although the primary vote slipped a little on the 2007 figures, it was still enough to get them over the line comfortably. But it wasn't a good result, because by-elections, especially late in the electoral cycle, are traditionally seen as opportunities for a protest vote against the government. True, there were no government candidates to protest against, but any genuine anti-government feeling should have translated itself into support for the Liberal alternative. This did not happen, so few Liberals were dancing in the streets. But it could have been worse; at least the voters did not punish the party for the extraordinary events of the previous three weeks, when they had been floundering around in search of their soul (or perhaps their arsehole).

Emboldened, Abbott announced that he had again been rummaging in the graveyard and had exhumed Howard's old press secretary, Tony O'Leary, who would once more haunt and harass the press gallery. It was a thought to make the old hands shudder, but not as much as Abbott's next announcement: border protection would be an issue at the next election.

As a bald statement this was unexceptionable; the influx of boat people had undeniably increased over the previous year, and the government's attempt to find a solution through cooperation with Indonesia had, so far at least, proved totally unsuccessful. Indeed, Kevin Rudd himself had been badly wounded by an incident in which an Australian customs vessel, the *Oceanic Viking*, had rescued seventy-eight Tamils from a boat floundering in Indonesian waters and delivered them to an Indonesian port, where they refused to disembark. The stand-off was eventually resolved when Australian officials struck a deal promising them speedy processing and resettlement and a host of side benefits, which Rudd insisted, preposterously, did not constitute special treatment. His constant repetition of this assertion went from being unbelievable to absurd to, finally, slightly demented.

Border protection could thus be seen as a legitimate political issue; but anyone who remembered 2001 knew that in the mouths of Liberal leaders it could also be code for race. And Abbott had made it clear that he saw the election as a no-holds-barred brawl which he would fight the same way as he had won his Oxford blue: 'No-style Abbott a real smasher,' read the report. 'He has no defence when going forward.' Abbott, it should also be remembered, was educated by Jesuits, who have been known to espouse the doctrine that the end can justify the means. He is not himself a racist; unlike John Howard he is comfortable working with people of all colours and creeds and has an excellent relationship with Aboriginal Australians. He is also a sincere, if belated, convert to the idea of multiculturalism. But desperate elections require desperate measures, and Abbott was quite capable of dog-whistling to what he knew were the worst instincts of Australians if he believed there were votes in it. It was a depressing note on which to end the year.

> *Just shut up and entertain me, meat puppet!*
> —Bradley Woodford

 2.

AS THE CUCKOO AND THE JONQUIL announce the arrival of spring, as the cicada and the shark attack are the harbingers of summer, so the first Newspoll ushers in election year. The revelation came on 19 January, and like most important oracles it was not easy to interpret. On the one hand it showed a swing away from Labor; the primary vote fell by 3 per cent, to a still-healthy 40 per cent. But there was little joy for the Coalition, because it picked up nothing: the gains went to Greens and independents. Certainly the margin on the two-party-preferred figure narrowed, but at 54–46 it was still in landslide territory.

On a personal level Tony Abbott could take some comfort. Kevin Rudd's satisfaction rating had tumbled to a mere 58 per cent and those dissatisfied had risen to 34; the net positive – 18 – was just about the smallest since the election. Admittedly Abbott's own net positive was only 5 – 40 for to 35 against, with an awful lot of don't knows and don't want to knows – but at least it was a big improvement on Malcolm Turnbull's last numbers. And it showed the faithful were coming back; Coalition voters who had been unhappy with Turnbull embraced

Abbott. This was just as well, because Labor voters who had quite liked Turnbull loathed his replacement.

Abbott returned to Mollymook on the New South Wales south coast to be photographed on a surfboard out behind the breakers. 'You won't find Kevin Rudd out here,' he boasted, and indeed you wouldn't. The prime minister was busy being states-manlike – even regal. He had decided to mark the lead-up to Australia Day by holding a sort of progress around the nation to allow as many of his adoring subjects as possible to see him in the flesh, or at least on the television news. And to prove that he was still a caring, sharing human person he launched the afore-mentioned children's book. Barnaby Joyce helped with the publicity by producing a parody. Much space was devoted by the media to identifying the book's villain, a scruffy animal called Chewy. I recalled that John Howard's own colleagues christened him The Rodent, for his habit of gnawing away at his various leaders. And of course there was Munchin' Minchin. Well, it was just a thought. Rudd also announced that he would resume his weekly appearances on Channel Seven's *Sunrise* program, a clear signal that he was slipping into pre-election mode. It was not revealed whether his old co-star, Joe Hockey, would also be making a comeback.

This feel-good stuff was clearly getting on Tony Abbott's nerves. He himself was going weekly on Channel Nine – not solo to answer patsy questions but head to head with his old rival, Julia Gillard. And he could do with the practice; he had cast himself as Action Man, the Great Opposer, but the govern-ment was giving him hardly anything to oppose. True, Rudd did mention that the task of reducing the deficit had become harder since Howard had increased government spending by amounts unthought of since the Whitlam era, and Abbott had responded in righteous but somewhat incoherent wrath, but by and large what the media know as the silly season was just that: silly. So Abbott decided to pick up the pace and came at Rudd from a totally unexpected direction. He proclaimed that he would move a private member's bill aimed at overturning the Queensland government's Wild Rivers legislation.

Premier Anna Bligh had announced that the Archer, Lockhart and Stewart river systems of Cape York would join six others as gazetted wild rivers where development deemed destructive to the environment would be banned. The declaration outraged the Aboriginal residents, in particular their charismatic leader Noel Pearson and his brother Gerhardt, who had been putting together plans for the development of the area to provide employment and eventual self-sufficiency. Pearson denounced the decision as 'foreclosing on a future for our people ... the state cannot rip the future out from under indigenous children's feet.'

Bligh denied that this would be the effect of the law; development of a sensitive and sustainable kind would still be welcome. But there was no doubt that the gazettal severely limited the Pearsons' options and interposed another layer of bureaucracy between them and the land, which was found by the High Court's 1996 *Wik* decision to be in traditional indigenous ownership.

There was a certain irony in the fact that the *Wik* decision was largely gutted by Abbott's mentor, John Howard, and that Abbott was now proposing effectively to reinstate it. But unlike Howard, Abbott had credibility on indigenous issues. Indeed it could be argued that no politician in the federal parliament was better qualified to argue the Aboriginal case for Cape York.

Not only was Abbott a personal friend of the Pearsons, he was also a regular visitor to the peninsula and had done volunteer work at the troubled community of Aurukun at the mouth of the Archer River and inland at Coen. His private member's bill might have a tinge of political opportunism about it, but at least he knew what he was talking about.

Furthermore, although such a bill would almost certainly trigger a constitutional challenge, it was one the Commonwealth would probably win. The Opposition's legal affairs spokesman, the lawyer George Brandis, made a convincing case for it in an article in the *Australian*. He noted the similarities to the 1983 case involving Tasmania's Franklin River dam, which the Commonwealth won, and suggested that much the same arguments would apply, but in the Queensland case they would be even more clear cut.

The Commonwealth could invoke not only its constitutional power to make laws for Aboriginal people but also its external affairs power; in 2009 Australia signed the United Nations Declaration on the Rights of Indigenous Peoples, which among other things provided that 'indigenous peoples have the right to own, use, develop and control the lands, territories and resources they possess by reason of traditional ownership or traditional occupation.' At the time, of course, Abbott and Brandis had vigorously opposed the government's move. Now it looked rather handy.

There was never any chance that the bill would be passed; despite Abbott's predictable plea for a bipartisan approach, Kevin Rudd was not about to overrule the embattled Labor premier of his home state, especially if it involved setting what could be a far-reaching and potentially embarrassing precedent. But opposing the bill brought its own problems.

One of Rudd's first commitments as prime minister was to 'close the gap' between indigenous and non-indigenous Australians. By refusing Abbott's challenge to do something concrete and practical, and which had the support of some of Australia's most active and respected Aboriginal leaders, he risked being seen as putting political considerations ahead of good policy, and worse, of joining Bligh in sacrificing legitimate Aboriginal interests for more electorally valuable Green support. In addition, there was the wedge: the issue set the supporters of Aboriginal rights and the greenies, two groups that traditionally support Labor, against each other. Labor's own people denounced the whole thing as a stunt, but they could hardly deny it was a bloody good one.

And it didn't end there. Abbott also called for the Feds to take over the Murray–Darling Basin; in spite of Rudd's assurance that he had reached agreement with the states, another unholy row had developed between New South Wales and South Australia, with Victoria and Queensland ready to jump in the moment their own interests were threatened. Abbott took the high ground: this vital environmental issue could not wait until Rudd's agreement took effect in 2012 or whenever; he should act now, even taking the matter to a referendum if necessary. To underline his green credentials, Abbott proposed a permanent 'green workforce' be created to tackle urgent matters as they came up.

He even got involved in the whaling controversy: with the Japanese whalers and the conservationists of the *Sea Shepherd* in open conflict in the Antarctic, Abbott demanded action. Rudd should go to the International Court of Justice as he had promised, or admit defeat. He himself favoured sending the hapless *Oceanic Viking* south to interpose itself between the warring parties. Or perhaps he didn't; when his less excitable environment spokesman Greg Hunt joined in, it all got a bit confused. But at least Abbott was going in, as he had vowed he would, with all guns blazing.

The only problem was, exactly what were they blazing at? Abbott had been elected leader because of concerns that

Turnbull was moving the Liberal Party too far to the left, positioning it too close to Labor. Abbott was supposed to return it to its roots. Yet he had spent over a week talking about Aborigines and whales, the long-derided darlings of the latte-sipping lovey-doveys. In the meantime the great symbolic policy of WorkChoices had been replaced with Fair Work Australia; why had we not heard a sustained rant about this craven capitulation to union power? Come on, Tony. We all like a good stunt, but it will never replace the real thing.

For a lot of Australians the real thing was still climate change. The news that 2009 had been confirmed as the second-hottest year on record (and the hottest of all for the southern hemisphere) further reinforced the concerns of the believers. Since the ascension of Abbott the issue had become seriously politicised. While Labor voters were still overwhelmingly convinced by the science, conservatives were drifting into doubt, even denial. What had once been a bipartisan conviction that action was urgently needed was becoming a matter of personal ideology. The sceptics were increasingly well organised, well funded and well publicised; when in January it was found that a piece of speculation had been presented as scientific fact in a report of the Intergovernmental Panel on Climate Change (IPCC), they crowed that the whole of the science had been discredited. It hadn't, of course, and even the importation of Gibbering Lord Monckton of Brenchley, an updated version of Screaming Lord Sutch, was considered unconvincing, especially when it was pointed out that while Monckton's calculations proved that global warming wasn't happening, they also proved that there had never been an ice age. Initially he was shunned by the Opposition. Gibbering Lord Monckton was considered too far out for Tony Abbott, and even for Barnaby Joyce – or he was until parliament resumed and Abbott invited the mad viscount to his office. Presumably after the release of his own climate-change policy, nothing and no one was too silly.

Nonetheless, the issue was no longer one on which Rudd and his ministers could coast. They were ready to reintroduce the ETS as soon as parliament resumed, but there was no real expectation that it would be passed; any potential floor-crossers from the Coalition side had been hauled into line and the independents, especially the flat-earther Steve Fielding, were not for turning. The numbers were simply not there. And then the Greens, of all people, moved to break the impasse. With a great (self-trumpeted) fanfare, they returned to the climate-change debate – and about bloody time.

Many on the left, including some of the deepest greens, had been shocked and dismayed at their intransigence during the last year, and in particular at its chaotic conclusion. From the very beginning, Senators Bob Brown, Christine Milne and their three colleagues had rejected the government's agenda out of hand. It was, they insisted, a worthless travesty of what was really required – a pusillanimous and inadequate response to a worldwide crisis. From a rigorous scientific point of view they may well have been right, but politics has never been a rigorous, scientific business. It is the art of the possible, about least-worst solutions achieved through compromise.

Rudd's approach was a long way from perfect, but it was a start, an attempt to ease the nation into a new and potentially unpleasant way of life. His calculation, reinforced by the best research available, was that the public simply would not accept the radical tactics favoured by the Greens, or even the more considered measures suggested by his own chief adviser, Ross Garnaut. He wanted to achieve at least a rough consensus, not only among the voters, but among the major stakeholders.

That meant bringing everyone, including the polluting industries, inside the tent. Of course there would always be recalcitrants, but as long as they could be portrayed as a perverse or self-seeking minority, there was a good chance of progress. Above all, he wanted political bipartisanship, which was why his final bill was very similar to the outline John Howard had taken to the electorate in 2007.

And he very nearly succeeded; right up until the last gasp it had appeared that Malcolm Turnbull would deliver enough senators to pass his emissions trading scheme and thus lock the foundations for real change into place. But the Greens wanted no part of it. They said they were open to negotiation, but their starting point was a target which would have strained the limits of many in the Labor Party, much less the Coalition. And in any case, the hard fact was that the Greens could not offer Rudd what he needed: the numbers to get the bill – any bill – passed. There were only five of them; Rudd needed seven. Any formula which would satisfy the Greens was bound to be opposed by the Liberals, even under Turnbull, and the Nationals were already off the planet. Thus Rudd would have needed both independents. Nick Xenophon might have been open to persuasion, but Steve Fielding was a hopeless case. Rudd's only hope was the Liberals, which meant more compromise, not more bravado.

Ironically, even after Turnbull was rolled, the Greens could still have saved the day: two Liberals were prepared to cross the floor, and if the Greens had seized the moment, as many of their supporters urged, a flawed but basic ETS would have become law; the foundation for more determined action would be in place. But the Greens preferred to preserve their ideological impregnability, and delivered precisely nothing. As Gough Whitlam was fond of remarking, the impotent are always pure – and, he might have added, frequently vice versa.

Brown and Milne then had a Damascene conversion to reality, proposing what they described as an interim scheme to break the deadlock. The idea was a two-year price on carbon of $20 per tonne; the proceeds would go towards incentives for alternative energy and compensating low-income households – and not to the polluting industries, who would receive free permits under the government scheme.

This was in line with the original Garnaut report and therefore had a certain credibility. But it was undeniably a compromise – even the Greens didn't claim it would do much to reduce the actual rate of emissions. The best they could predict was that at least it might stop them from increasing, and perhaps, just perhaps, bring them down by a percentage point or two. This was a long way behind the government's own minimum target of 5 per cent reductions, about which they had been so contemptuous. But again, it would be a start.

Unfortunately all the old political constraints still applied. In the Senate as it stood, a Labor–Greens alliance was still two votes short of a majority. Yet the Greens' proposal was just about the only concrete plan for action on the table. Clearly something would have to be done about it.

But first there was Australia Day – Survival Day, as indigenous Australians now call it. And they're right; 26 January is something that has to be survived.

There is a land of summer skies
Where everyone gets rich who tries
And politicians don't tell lies, no porky pies.
And there's no poverty or crime
Or graft or vice or sleaze or slime
And all the buses run on time
Australia, Australia, Austray-hay-lia.

Or something like that.

In 2010 Australia Day was vigorously pushed as a time for unbridled rejoicing: 'Barbecue like you've never barbecued before,' 'Man your eskies,' exhorted the official advertising. In other words, eat a lot of dead animals and get extremely pissed. But Kevin Rudd, as ever, seemed determined to rain on the patriotic parade. True, he urged us to celebrate this sacred day (the day we officially became a British penal colony, you little beauty!) and extolled the great Australian virtues of the fair go and can do – but he also added that we'll bloody well need them, as we're heading towards a future full of doom and gloom.

Rudd had spent the week leading up to Australia Day on a sort of prime ministerial progress around the country, ringing his bell and proclaiming that the end of the world was nigh. He was not the first to note that the Australian population was rapidly ageing; even Peter Costello had roused himself for long enough to make the observation. But instead of urging a bit of jolly copulation as the solution, Rudd adopted the persona of Boxer, the horse in George Orwell's *Animal Farm*.

'My fellow Australians,' he intoned, 'we must all work harder.' And longer. And more productively.

Treasury Secretary Ken Henry joined in the jeremiad by suggesting that we might all like to pay more taxes as well, but Wayne Swan promptly put the kibosh on that. Nonetheless, the tone of the message was clear: yet more blood and toil, tears and sweat. The health system alone was utterly out of control, both in terms of administration and expense. Reforms would soon be announced, but let no one imagine that they would be cheap or easy. Man was born to trouble as the sparks fly upward, and he could see plenty of pain and suffering ahead.

It was an unlikely pitch for an election year, but it could be a hard one for the Opposition to match. Oppositions need to be able to promise better times ahead and plenty of goodies to make them happen. Rudd's theme would portray such promises as reckless and ultimately destructive; the government would campaign on economic responsibility. Boring but safe – rather like the man himself.

If Rudd's message was depressing, at least it was inclusive; the bad news was for everyone. Tony Abbott, on the other hand, decided that Australia Day was the right occasion for an address on immigration and border protection. Abbott, like Rudd, was a Big Australia man; both were in favour of bolstering the population through an aggressive immigration program and both espoused border protection as a necessary corollary. But from this point their messages became very different.

Abbott started with the claim that Australians were worried about the number of boat people seeking asylum, the implication being that if they weren't then they should be, and he was going to make sure they were. He didn't even attempt to explain why a few thousand wretched and desperate refugees in boats constituted an existential threat to the country's future while the vastly greater number who arrived by air could be safely ignored. That they were was simply a given, part of the Australian psyche.

'Unfortunately there are no easy ways to deter people who want to force themselves on Australia,' he averred, as if this was a crisis, a matter of national survival.

And in case we still hadn't got the message, he reverted to the 2001 election slogan of his old mentor: 'John Howard's declaration about Australians controlling who comes to this country resonated because it struck most people as self-evidently and robustly true,' Abbott said proudly. Unsurprisingly, Abbott's fond recollections of the time were not shared by the human-rights advocates (namby-pamby bleeding hearts) who accused him of muddled thinking and trying to reinvigorate the bitterness of those times. 'This is the language of *Tampa*,' said the president of the Refugee Council of Australia, John Gibson; it was perhaps the strongest condemnation he could imagine.

More telling and probably more hurtful was a gentler rebuke from Professor Patrick McGorry, the psychiatrist named official Australian of the Year. McGorry had already said he planned to speak to his fellow title-holder Kevin Rudd about the need to close down the detention centres, which he described as 'factories for mental illness.' He praised Rudd for his more compassionate approach and added that he hoped Abbott could be persuaded to take a similar attitude. He definitely wanted the issue off the table before the election campaign proper got under way. The tone was diplomatic, but the message was unmistakable. Migrant organisations also objected to some of Abbott's other assertions, including the suggestion that they took the 'great prize' of Australian citizenship too lightly and that some recent immigrants seemed resistant to Australian notions of equality. Marion Le, a human-rights advocate, said Abbott was just wrong, and that his language was divisive and offensive. It was a large and concerted spray, which if nothing else confirmed that Abbott had simply made the wrong speech for Australia Day.

Even more mortifying was the news that the magazine *Zoo Weekly* had named the Opposition leader its Un-Australian of the Year – not for his speeches, ideas or attitudes, but for the heinous crime of bringing Speedos into disrepute. While at the other end of the spectrum his arch-rival had been named by the organisation he considered his greatest ally – the Murdoch Press – as its favourite son. Well, for a day at least.

This seems altogether too gloomy a note on which to leave our national day, so let's conclude with something a little more upbeat. Like our flag, our national anthem has always been a problem. Most find it merely second-rate, while others cringe with embarrassment whenever they hear it – both the tune and, more especially, the words. However, attempts at a substitute have generally been even more woeful. Literary critics contend that the problem is partly one of assonance; Australia is a hard country to celebrate in song and verse because the only obvious rhyme is 'failure.' I regard this attitude as defeatist, as the following stirring ditty should show:

Australia! You're not a failure
As long as there's azalea to espalier.
In your regalia
Bright as a dahlia
We'll hail ya not bewail ya our Australia.

So perhaps things weren't quite as bad as Kevin Rudd made out. On the other hand, perhaps they were even worse. But at least it was the end of the silly season.

> *The day I need a television puppet to teach my children what's right and what's wrong, I'll bow out as a mother.* —ELINOR SMITH

★ 3.

OR IT WOULD HAVE BEEN if Tony Abbott had not told the *Women's Weekly* that he would advise his daughters to sit on it until they were married. Actually, if he had put it as straightforwardly as that there probably wouldn't have been much of a fuss. Some might have derided him as a bit old-fashioned (or, as his eighteen-year-old daughter Frances put it, 'a lame, gay, churchy loser') but a lot of traditional parents might have shrugged in mute agreement.

However, Abbott being Abbott, he had to take it further. After all, the *Weekly* was doing an extensive piece on his favourite subject – himself – and indeed on his favourite aspects of it: ethics and beliefs, creed and credo. So Abbott felt constrained to add that virginity was a gift from God to a woman, and the most precious gift she could give to a man. By way of later explanation he insisted that he wasn't preaching – this was simply the advice that he would give to his own three daughters, although given that two of them had already reached adulthood it could be seen as a touch patronising. But no one really believed him. The worst fears of the moderates, both inside and outside the Liberal Party, were confirmed: Captain Catholic was back in charge. The Mad Monk just couldn't help himself; he was incapable of drawing the line between public policy and private morals. And in Australia, this was always going to be a bummer.

I was irresistibly reminded of an occasion many years ago when a group of journalists was dragged by Gough Whitlam to the archaeological site of Tenochtitlan, where a guide lectured them on Aztec culture. The hacks would much rather have been drinking around the swimming pool but at least one of them perked up when the guide got to the midsummer sacrifice.

'And every year the priest would rip the heart out of a virgin and display it to the people.'

'Hang on a minute,' said the inquirer. 'This happened every year, right?'

'Yes sir, every year at the solstice of midsummer.'

'And the victim had to be a virgin, right?'

'Yes sir, a maiden untouched by man.'

'Well, geez, you'd think that after a few years the girls would have got the message.'

Abbott received more support than he probably expected; talkback radio ended up slightly in his favour thanks to a blitz by women of a certain age (and possibly also a certain religion). Kevin Rudd sensibly laid low and said nothing, and his deputy Julia Gillard confined herself to the terse observation that Australian women could make their own choices and did not want to be lectured by Tony Abbott. Even this was too much for the Liberals' normally sensible George Brandis, who said that Gillard had no right to talk about families because she didn't have one herself. The quick response was that Gillard was not talking about families but about Tony Abbott, and that Brandis would presumably also disqualify the pope and all celibate clergy from the debate; indeed, perhaps he should disqualify himself from discussing women and children since he did not have a womb.

The argument soon moved on to Abbott's hypocrisy, which he at least acknowledged; after all, he could hardly deny it. Rather sheepishly he admitted that when his daughters said to him, 'But Daddy, you did all those things yourself,' he had replied, 'Well, yes, I did.' Thus when he claimed that he was urging restraint upon young men as well as young women, there was a certain amount of coarse laughter. But the more serious underlying complaint was about the idea that a woman's virginity, and therefore presumably her entire sex life, could be regarded as no more than a gift to a man. The issue died a natural death in the media, but the memory of that piece of unbridled misogyny lingered on.

Fortunately for Abbott, there were other distractions: the launch of Julia Gillard's long-awaited My School website was marred by several technical hitches, and also by some embarrassing misreporting, but these mistakes were rectifiable and forgivable. Harder to counter was the complaint that by isolating test results from the totality of a school's culture, the site gave a seriously misleading impression of a school's overall quality. Gillard insisted that parents had a right to know and that the main purpose of the tests was to identify schools that need extra help.

The teachers, in particular, were not convinced; they claimed that publication of the tests would inevitably lead to league tables of schools, with the losers denigrated and humiliated without any serious examination of their problems. But it proved extremely popular with the general public, and as there were many more of them than there were members of the teachers' unions, Gillard's initiative could be counted a political success.

Certainly in the world outside Canberra it was seen as cementing her credentials for leadership if St Kevin was ever taken to his ancestors or, more probably, assumed directly into heaven. The left was partially appeased by the promise that the website would soon be expanded to include all sources of schools' funding, a move vigorously opposed by the private schools. In fact the public sector emerged from the exercise far better than most had anticipated; in many areas the local state school comprehensively out-performed its expensive private rival. Further, the firm identification of truly disadvantaged schools meant that there was now no rational excuse for persisting with the absurd funding policy Rudd had inherited from Howard – if indeed there ever had been. However, change was always going to be controversial, and the last thing Rudd wanted was a controversial start to a year in which the government would try and portray itself as steady and middle-of-the-road.

The upside was that it was a concrete achievement, even a reform – and not many of those had actually been delivered. Rudd showed that he was aware of this in a lengthy interview on the *7.30 Report*. He noted water reform in the Murray–Darling Basin and improvements to the hospital system as areas in which important agreements had been negotiated with the states and many changes had already been made. But he also acknowledged that more was needed on the scoreboard; the awful example of Barack Obama's collapse in popularity was only an ocean away.

Fortunately the early statistics were looking good. Unemployment may have peaked, and while inflation was gathering pace and would certainly trigger some interest-rate rises in the course of the year, even this could be spun as good news: as a result of Australia's soft passage through the global financial crisis, our recovery was proceeding faster than anticipated, and certainly faster than the rest of the industrialised world. The latest International Monetary Reform report had revised its forecast for Australia's 2010 growth rate from 2.0 to 2.5 per cent. The government had proven itself to be a safe pair of hands, entitled to the high ground in any debate on economic management, and the Opposition's line about extravagant government spending and wasted stimulus money was simply not credible.

And speaking of credibility, we were still waiting for the Opposition's cost-free policy on climate change. Abbott and Greg Hunt had dropped a few hints: the idea of returning carbon to the soil, once seen as a breakthrough by Malcolm Turnbull, was going to figure large in the mixture. But given that Treasury had already assessed that idea as producing very little bang for a great many bucks, there would have to be more.

Abbott opened his sales pitch by trying to lay the issue down: Rudd was simply wrong in claiming that climate change was the great economic and political challenge of the age, he told a Young Liberals convention; why, even a temperature rise of four degrees would be no big deal. In fact, four degrees was twice what the science considered manageable: the general consensus was that such a rise would precipitate world-wide famine, huge rises in the sea level, a pandemic of tropical disease and catastrophic changes to weather patterns. No big deal? Any hope that Abbott was prepared to be part of the mainstream debate evaporated faster than Lake Eyre. So fortunately we had already been thoroughly disillusioned when the policy finally hit the deck.

To call it an anti-climax would be to heap it with unde-served praise. Indeed, to call it a policy at all would be over-stating the reality: it was closer to something you might find scrawled on the back of a beer mat after a long night on the turps.

Kevin Rudd dismissed it as a con job, but even on that level it was a pretty sloppy piece of work; a decent con requires at least some attention to detail to make it credible. My favourite description came from the *Sydney Morning Herald*'s Peter Hartcher, who suggested that it was a fig leaf – a little bit of greenery to hide the horrible nakedness of the Coalition over the whole issue. Or, of course, we could always fall back on Abbott's own robust phraseology: it was absolute crap.

The mere fact that the scheme was being welcomed by the heavy polluters was surely enough to establish its ineffectiveness. For them, as Abbott boasted, it would be business as usual. With no cap proposed for Australia's carbon emissions, there would be nothing to stop them continuing and even expanding their operations indefinitely. Indeed, they would be encouraged to do so: if an electricity generator, for example, wanted to build a new plant, one that would double its overall emissions, that would be fine as long as the new plant was not any dirtier than the ones the company was already operating. And if it turned out to be mildly cleaner, thereby bringing down the average intensity of the company's emissions, there would be a reward for building it.

This was the centrepiece of Abbott's reduction strategy: the actual volume of emissions didn't matter, but any individual polluter who showed signs of improvement would receive an elephant stamp, a remaindered copy of *Battlelines* and some unspecified financial incentive – to be determined through consultation with the polluters themselves, as would any penalty imposed for an increase in the intensity of emissions. Given the improvements to technology at all levels, the need for this stick was highly unlikely. On the other hand, the chances of

Abbott's carrot leading to the reduction of 5 per cent by 2020 to which he was committed – or any reduction at all – were also pretty slender. Barnaby Joyce said we could rely on greed to make it work, but then, Joyce was having a lot of trouble distinguishing trillions from billions, and even millions. Not a good look for a potential finance minister.

But wait, there was more. Farmers would be encouraged to bury carbon in the soil, although there was no proven way of measuring how much carbon they buried, let alone the logistics of how to bury it. And we would plant trees, say 20 million of them. We didn't know where or when, but we would plant trees; everyone agreed that this was an unambiguously good thing to do, as long as we didn't plant them where farmers didn't want them. And we would put solar cells on people's roofs, ignoring the fact that this had been shown to be the least cost-effective way of reducing emissions of them all. This would all cost about $10 billion and we didn't know where the money was coming from, but hey, we could cut foreign aid or sack a few public servants – at least that was Barnaby Joyce's version. Abbott said it wouldn't be like that at all. He didn't know quite what it would be like, but we'd be told once he'd worked it out. Now, wasn't 'direct action' simpler and more effective than an emissions trading scheme?

Well no, actually. According to every economic model produced, not just in Australia but around the world, the only way to get serious about reducing carbon emissions was to put a price on carbon; even the Greens now accepted this. There was still debate about whether a straightforward tax was superior to a market-based cap-and-trade system, but the need for some kind of pricing mechanism was as unarguable as climate change itself. But then, Abbott was not too certain about that, either. Kevin Rudd claimed that Abbott had changed his stance on climate change more times than he had changed his undies, which is probably unfair; as a cyclist, Abbott has always been meticulous about the condition of his jock strap. But it was certainly true that his climate-change policy was not that of a politician who was providing a considered response to a genuine problem.

Within forty-eight hours the government had produced an opinion from the Department of Climate Change that the Abbott plan would actually increase emissions by some 13 per cent by 2020. Abbott demanded to see the modelling and insisted that his own experts were better; he added, rather alarmingly, that his policy was based on the reduction plan pioneered by the New South Wales Labor government, hardly the most admired of role models. But the fact was that the policy was so vague and incomplete that it was impossible to evaluate properly. All that could sensibly be said was that the underlying concept had been universally dismissed as expensive and inadequate, and for that reason had never really been tried. There was still a chance that it might work; but then, there was still a chance that pigs might fly. The Opposition leader ended the week by pronouncing that the department was wrong, the economists were wrong, and of course Rudd was wrong, and incidentally even Barnaby Joyce was wrong; in fact everyone was wrong except him. The advocacy group Get Up! immediately announced plans for a huge billboard at Sydney Airport with the message: 'Tony, abstinence is not a climate option!'

Still, even Abbott's severest critics had to admit that there had been one useful spin-off: Kevin Rudd started to speak clearly about his own plan. His ETS was suddenly reduced from several pages of jargon and waffle to a simple grab: we put a cap on emissions; the polluters pay; and households get compensated for any price rises. Abbott's policy does none of the above. End of story. Actually, it was rather more complicated and less ideal than that, but at least Rudd was now making it sound comprehensible. He was not, however, making it acceptable to his opponents in the Senate. So what next?

Rudd had always insisted that doing nothing was not an acceptable response to this great moral, economic and political challenge, but, as Abbott pointed out, the government appeared to have no Plan B. Penny Wong's discussions with the Greens suddenly took on real political significance. Somewhat strangely, the Greens were also talking to Greg Hunt, although they had been among the first to pour scorn on the 'direct action' approach. Perhaps they really were going mainstream.

Climate change dominated the first week of the parliamentary sitting, and it was over climate change that the great divide was opened. But it wasn't the only game in town. There was the revelation that the unsuccessful attempt to get a private consortium together to run the national broadband network had cost the taxpayers some $17 million and the tenderers themselves another $13 million – an awful lot of money down the gurgler for a government that was planning its election campaign around the theme of economic responsibility. That was the bad news. The good news was that Barack Obama was to pay us a visit in March, to have a chat to his new best friend Kevin, and Kevin couldn't wait. While Obama might be a bit on the nose in his home country, he was still a folk hero in Australia.

And there was also a lot of equivocal news, which the government would have the opportunity to shape for its own ends. First was the Intergenerational Report, the document that had been lurking behind all Kevin Rudd's exhortations about the need to increase productivity and the urgency of health reform. The report wasn't as depressing as some of its predecessors had been. Australia still faced an ageing population with a proportionately declining workforce, but the decline was less drastic than previously feared. Nonetheless, we were all going to have to work, not necessarily harder, but definitely smarter and probably longer. The doom and gloom had lifted slightly, but there was still plenty to go around. The invaluable Ross Gittins in the *Sydney Morning Herald* pointed out that the real problem was not the ageing population itself but the increasing cost of healthcare: the technology was getting more expensive and more and more people were demanding access to it. And their steadfast refusal to pay for it through tax increases didn't make the problem any simpler.

Of course the numbers were decidedly rubbery: Treasury forecasts have been notoriously inaccurate even in the short term, and here the boffins were purporting to tell us what was going to happen in 2050, when most if not all would be securely dead. The treasurer, Wayne Swan, himself admitted that a lot could happen between now and then and that nothing, not least a population of 36 million, was set in stone.

That figure alone was enough to spark a furious debate between the advocates of a big Australia and an expanded migration program, and those who saw the infrastructure, social cohesion and above all the water supply of the continent already overstretched. Rudd, of course, was on the side of the big country; he always had been. And so had Tony Abbott, but given his promise to oppose Rudd on everything, his support for a bipartisan policy could no longer be taken for granted.

Yet again, Rudd threatened to take tough decisions. The more experienced listeners, who had long since ceased holding their breath in expectation, nodded encouragingly; the time was approaching to do something about the hospital system. And the polls showed that the Opposition line about Rudd being all talk and no action was finally starting to bite.

The Newspoll released that same day confirmed Labor's worst fears; the Coalition had taken a narrow lead on primary voters for the first time since well before the 2007 election. Green preferences would still get the government comfortably home, the two-party-preferred still showed Labor with a lead of 52–48, and Rudd was still more than doubling Abbott's score as preferred prime minister. There was no crisis, yet – but overnight Labor had gone from being a rolled-gold certainty to a mere short-priced favourite, and the bookies said that serious money was coming in to back the Coalition. Rudd used the numbers to warn his party room that Labor could lose; all it would take was two or three voters in every hundred to change their minds, and the game was over. He pointed out, rightly, that governments traditionally 'lost some skin' at their first-term election: Bob Hawke in 1984 and John Howard in 1998 had both run it very close indeed. He did not add that, in the final count, both had won and gone on to greater things, nor did he mention that Australia had not had a one-term government since Jimmy Scullin ran up against the Great Depression.

But he did include his colleagues in his general demand for a new year's resolution. Like the rest of the populace, they needed to work harder and smarter to get the Labor story across. Why, even he had room to improve – he would have to get his message across more clearly. And to his credit, he immediately went out and did so with his severely edited spiel about climate change. Labor apparatchiks were surprised and impressed, but privately expressed some doubts as to whether their glorious leader would be able to break the habit of a lifetime when it came to explaining the ins and outs of economic management, which no one doubted would be the real battle-ground leading up to polling day.

Abbott had certainly accepted that this would be the case, and had already unveiled one snappy slogan: he would reduce the pressure on household budgets. But hadn't we heard something like this before? Ah, yes, in 2004: 'Ease the squeeze,' the ill-fated war cry of the worse-fated Mark Latham.

For Tony Abbott and his reluctant Treasury spokesman Joe Hockey, the action was in the supermarkets. Abbott had worked for John Hewson during the 1993 'GST' election, and he had seen the way Labor had destroyed both the leader and his policy through a retail blitz: an apparently endless series of nagging questions about how the new tax would affect a specific range of goods for a targeted range of voters. He was now applying the same technique to what he still insisted on calling 'Mr Rudd's great big new tax on everything' and had already identified a crowd of losers, for whom the compensation announced by the government for its ETS scheme would prove inadequate.

It also tied in nicely with another attack, the one on Fair Work Australia, which, unsurprisingly, was having a few teething problems in its first couple of months. Once again there were losers; it appeared that some workers would in fact be worse off as a result of the changes. A poignant case was that of children who could no longer get after-school jobs, as the new minimum shift was three hours rather than two; if they couldn't start until 4 p.m., the shops would close before they could complete a shift. But there were other anomalies as well, and we were treated to the bizarre sight of the Opposition spokesman, Eric Abetz, one of the fathers of WorkChoices, suddenly emerging as the workers' friend.

Abetz formed an unlikely alliance with Dean Mighell of the

Electrical Trades Union, who in 2007 had called John Howard a skid mark on the bedsheet of history and been drummed out of the Labor Party at Rudd's insistence as a result. Mighell now accused both the government and the ACTU of ratting on the workers, a sentiment Abetz enthusiastically endorsed. But Abetz was rather more friendly with the bosses, particularly the mining giants of the Pilbara, who were forced to negotiate with the unions for the first time in a decade and hated every moment of it. The problem was that any gesture of sympathy for their plight could be seen as confirmation of the government's line that the Coalition really wanted to bring back Work-Choices, which was still electoral poison. It was much safer to take up the case of the schoolchildren.

All in all it had been a pretty fair first week of parliament for the Opposition, although not quite as good as the *Australian* made out. On Saturday the indefatigable Dennis Shanahan hit the front page with a piece explaining that the government's desperate attacks on Abbott's climate policy (the Emissions Reduction Fund, or ERF, as it had now become) had doomed Rudd's own ETS; if the logic was not quite clear, the intention certainly was.

Inside, someone called Brendan O'Neill accused the believers in climate change of elevating their science 'above democracy'; he apparently felt that if the sceptics could whip up a majority in a plebiscite, that would fix the problem. Similar votes could be used to establish that the earth was flat and the moon made of green cheese. O'Neill had obviously never read Henrik Ibsen's great play *An Enemy of the People*, in which the rational protagonist is forced to fall back on the slogan, 'The majority is always wrong.'

To cap it off, the paper's 'Cut and Paste' column took union-ist Paul Howes to task for calling the *Australian* 'the third member of the Coalition.' Why, the column gasped indignantly, only a fortnight ago the paper had anointed Kevin Rudd as its Australian of the Year. It was obvious that this meaningless accolade was going to be trotted out to counter every well-merited accusation of partisanship between now and the election. Abby and Jasper would be disappointed.

Of course, the news was not all good for the Coalition. Frontier Economics, the forum that had put the ERF together for Abbott, admitted publicly that it was never intended as anything more than a stop-gap; obviously it would do nothing to solve the long-term problem of carbon emissions. And this, of course, was Abbott's problem; he had called the science absolute crap, but he wanted the voters to believe that he was taking the issue seriously, and he was prepared to throw billions of taxpayer dollars at it. Yet by any proper analysis, his plan wouldn't work. Was there a little question of consistency here?

Abbott continued to brazen it out, insisting that whether or not you believed in climate change, the policy was good for the environment, which was true, up to a point; it certainly had some potential benefits for farmers, and Abbott opined that rural and regional Labor members would be terrified at the prospect of arguing the merits of the ETS and the ERF once Barnaby Joyce appeared in their electorates.

Ah, yes, Barnaby Joyce. The Blooperman of the National Party was getting off a few good one-liners, but the uncooperative media insisted on finding his gaffes both funnier and more newsworthy. His National Press Club speech on the day after Abbott's policy launch was generally derided as a disaster, and although Abbott manfully played it down with waffle about how his shadow finance minister was still on a learning curve, no one really believed that Joyce's political skills would rise significantly above those of Forrest Gump.

The dilemma was that his greatest – indeed, probably his only – political asset was his naturalness; muzzle him and you'd lose everything you wanted to keep, but leave him unmuzzled and you could expect an endless string of blunders which not only provided the government and the media with hours of good clean fun, but totally undermined Abbott's already dubious claims to economic credibility. After all, Abbott was still getting over the appearance of his shadow treasurer, Joe Hockey, with a pink tutu, crown and fairy wand, as Abba's 'Dancing Queen' on daytime television. Fortunately Kevin Rudd was also back on the internet, caught wiping his nose on his hand as he stepped up to the dispatch box. It was unlikely to become a hit on the level of his meal of ear wax, but it was better than nothing. And the *Sydney Morning Herald*, of all papers, ran a picture of Rudd apparently going bald.

This was just what Abbott needed to go with the Nielsen poll announcing that the wheels had fallen off the ETS. After the briefest of glances at his ERF, the punters preferred it to Rudd's scheme by a margin of 45–39. On the Brendan O'Neill theory, this trashed all the scientists and economists in the land.

It also gave 'Professor' Paul Kelly the opportunity he, and indeed all of us, had been waiting for: the headline in the *Australian* reading 'Rudd's Decisive Test.' As I have noted before, there is nothing journalists love more than setting tests for politicians, having first appointed themselves as sole examiners and assessors. It gives them such a pleasing sense of moral and intellectual superiority. Kelly, a serial offender, now demanded that Rudd defend his ETS to the death; he must show political courage and conviction. It was, said Kelly – confirming the suspicion that he had spent too much time in the United States – a matter of character. If Rudd backed away and agreed to the Greens' compromise scheme, he would look weak and intimidated. It was the ETS or nothing. Kelly was careful not to mention that his own paper had spent much of the last twelve months diligently undermining support for the ETS and would presumably continue to do so.

Funnily enough, Ross Gittins in the *Sydney Morning Herald* agreed with Kelly's basic thesis, although Gittins put it rather less pompously: Rudd could stand and fight or he could cut and run. Unfortunately neither pundit had any ideas about how to manage the political fight. Malcolm Turnbull stepped in with a passionate defence of the ETS and a comprehensive rubbishing of Abbott's policy. It was a brilliant parliamentary performance, the speech that should have been made by Rudd, or Penny Wong, or Greg Combet, or someone – anyone – on the government side. But for all its dramatic impact, its political effect was zilch.

Perhaps the key political event of the session was the appearance of Rudd on the ABC's *Q&A* program, being grilled for an hour by an audience of 200 young Australians aged eighteen to twenty-five. This was the demographic that had swung decisively behind Rudd in 2007 and still favoured Labor by a margin of two to one. But the *Q&A* crowd established immediately that they were not to be taken for granted. They had attitude, and they voted. Moreover, at least a couple of them were young Libs, well primed for the occasion. Rudd kept his cool, but was widely judged to have lost the encounter badly. Perhaps it was the fact that there was no real news in it that annoyed journalists; even so, some of them made headlines out of Rudd's personal preference to raise the drinking age, although he made it clear that this was not government policy. He was assailed for being condescending and patronising, but also for treating his questioners as he treated the Canberra press gallery. Even Rudd at his hoitiest knew better than to patronise the press gallery, so perhaps the criticism was a little harsh. The cruellest comment was a line from Twitter which said that Rudd had been getting his own back on the sort of girls who had denied him sex in high school. Rudd, in the same forum, simply described the evening as 'a tough gig.' And it led to a tough week.

Things started promisingly, with Barnaby Joyce at it again. This time he announced gravely that Australia was about to go down the gurgler: debt was out of control.

'We are getting to the point where we can't repay it,' he told a startled nation. Rudd and Swan immediately slapped him down and Abbott and Hockey corrected him; the line was not only wildly irresponsible but utterly untenable. In relation to its economy, Australia's debt was just about the lowest in the world. To be precise, it was 15.9 per cent of GDP, compared to New Zealand's 27 per cent, the UK's 81.8 per cent and the USA's 83.9 per cent. Rudd and Swan demanded that Abbott sack Joyce as his finance spokesman, thereby ensuring that he would not do so; after all, it was Joyce who described himself as 'the gift that keeps on giving.' It was the truest thing he had ever said. But even Abbott had to draw the line somewhere. He refused to guarantee that Joyce would stay in his current job; instead, he hinted, the wild one might be sent around the rural and regional electorates, especially those held by Labor, to spread the good word (well, his word) about debt, tax, drought, fire, flood and locusts and all the other plagues Kevin Rudd was set to unleash on them.

Then Abbott himself took retail politics a step too far by talking about housewives ironing their husbands' shirts, which was not what most women wanted to hear. But that was about as good as it got for the government. Ministers found time to do a little governing: immigration minister Chris Evans announced an end to the racket by which overseas students could do a course in hairdressing and immediately become eligible for permanent residency. Indian students, already unhappy about a spate of what appeared to be racially based assaults, were now horrified to find that what they had been sold as a back-door method of immigration would guarantee them no more than an education – and not much of a one at that if they were clients of the fly-by-nighters that had sprung up to cash in on the rort. There was a muted outcry, but by and large the move was accepted as good, and overdue, policy.

Then Abbott fronted for a bit more direct action. The government had already announced its plan for eighteen weeks of paid maternity leave; Abbott gazumped the offer to six months, saying it should cover the full period of breastfeeding. Cynics saw this as a desperate attempt to regain some ground with the women's vote. The government said it was unafford-able, especially as the Opposition was still insisting that gov-ernment spending had to be curtailed because it was driving up interest rates, and was riffling through the speeches of Reserve Bank governor Glenn Stevens in the hope of finding some tenuous support for the claim. But at least it was a posi-tive move; after a couple of weeks of Barnaby Joyce, Abbott sorely needed one. And then suddenly the government pro-duced its own Barnaby – well, not quite; there was only one Barnaby. But Peter Garrett was the next best thing.

The environment minister had successfully kept as low a profile as his superhuman appearance and occasional returns to the rock stage made possible, but he was always seen as a potential loose cannon, a gifted amateur itching to play his strokes rather than a serious professional determined to hang on to his wicket at all costs. However, the breakthrough even-tually came not from any real recklessness on Garrett's part but because he was saddled with a program which was not ready to be implemented. The home insulation rebate scheme was conceived as part of the government's stimulus package as well as a way of enhancing its green credentials; there was not a moment to lose. So it was rushed out with little preparation. Installers were given crash training programs and suppliers grabbed whatever materials were to hand.

From the start there were stories of waste and mismanagement, even of downright fraud, but the government could and did live with these. In the context of defeating the global financial crisis, they could be dismissed as inconsequential; as a threat to public safety, they could not. It turned out that in some cases metal foil had been used as an insulating material and installed over live electric wiring, and that in a few of those cases the installation had been faulty; as a result, the roof space had become a fully charged capacitor, potentially lethal to the unwary householder. And indeed, no less than four installers had died on the job.

Their deaths could hardly be blamed on Garrett, although the Opposition gave it a try: Abbott actually implied that he was personally guilty of manslaughter. But the charge of negligence was harder to shrug off, especially when it became clear that Garrett's department had received thirteen warnings from state governments, unions and almost everyone else that the scheme was too big and cumbersome to be regulated effectively and of the dangers to both life and property. Now some 37,000 foil installations would need a safety check and the dodgy ones would have to be repaired. The total cost could amount to $50 million. After more than two long years the Opposition finally had visions of a ministerial scalp – or in Garrett's case, a giant bald pate.

Rudd was not prepared to lose Garrett; he had personally

demanded his inclusion in the ministry and remained convinced of his electoral value in spite of the disillusionment expressed by many on the left as their former idol drifted into the anonymity of mainstream politics. Moreover, Rudd was proud of his record; in more than two years he had only lost one minister. Joel Fitzgibbon had been forced to resign from the defence portfolio after failing to declare substantial gifts from the Chinese-Australian businesswoman Helen Liu, who was herself under investigation by Chinese authorities. Then his brother used his office to do some unauthorised lobbying. This was unquestionably a hanging offence, and Fitzgibbon was duly hung. But Garrett's case was less straightforward. Certainly he had presided over a bungled scheme, but the actual bungling was the fault of the installers; they had failed to observe normal industry safety standards. To say that he was utterly incompetent in the handling of his portfolio, as Abbott now did, was a bit rich; after all, Abbott had previously spoken about the difficulties of administering a large and complex department. Perhaps for this reason Abbott aimed his ritual censure motion not at Garrett for being incompetent but at Rudd for failing to sack him.

The Rudd-haters in the media showed no such restraint; the prospect of giving their arch-enemy a good populist savaging was simply too good to miss. Perhaps the most rabid response of all came from that good Catholic Miranda Devine, who went to the extent of inventing a whole new no-fault moral philosophy. In her column in the *Sydney Morning Herald*, Devine's obsessive hatred of green-left issues climaxed in what she called 'the burning batts fiasco,' which brought together those two notorious moral degenerates Kevin Rudd and Peter Garrett.

After a couple of dozen paragraphs of barely controlled bile, she summed up the situation in a quotation from a relative of one of the victims: 'If someone gives people the opportunity to be dodgy, they'll be dodgy.' This, she said, is the moral universe most people live in. And a very comfortable one it must be. In this universe you don't blame the dodgy installers who made the dodgy decisions that caused the accidents: you blame the government. Nothing's ever your own fault. So much for those silly old doctrines of free will, personal responsibility and the need to choose between right and wrong. The pope would be surprised.

Rudd shrugged it off, or at least attempted to. It was clear that the Opposition was not going to let up; they seemed to be getting a lot of powerful leaked information and there was almost certainly more to come. It was the kind of issue that politicians hate: not an earth-shaking catastrophe, a mega-tragedy too vast for the normal mind to encompass, but a nasty scandal of bungling and misadventure on a scale all too famil-iar to the average voter. What was worse, just about everyone had been approached to have their roof insulated, or knew someone who had. Rudd, with plenty of experience of such irritants from his time working for the Queensland state gov-ernment, must have realised it was a long way from over. But in the meantime he went back to talking about the surprisingly good employment statistics which had just been released; the optimists gloated that the government and the Reserve Bank had both been too cautious and we really were out of the woods.

But if we were, there was a depressing amount of ingrati-tude around the place. The *Australian* reported triumphantly: 'Business Losing Faith in Rudd.' Well, actually it wasn't all business but the Business Council of Australia's new president, Graham Bradley, who had never been much of a fan anyway. On the other side of the economy, the unions weren't all that happy either; the heavies of the CFMEU complained that there were still far too many vestiges of WorkChoices clogging up the system. If Rudd had deigned to reply he would no doubt have fallen back on his old formula: if both sides were unhappy with him, he must be doing the right thing. But it wasn't only those with logs to roll and axes to grind who were getting a bit toey. Rudd needed a big announcement of some kind, and although there were a few on the backburner, none was quite ready to unveil.

The first fortnight of the parliamentary session ended as it should have started, with Rudd's annual report on closing the gap between indigenous Australians and the rest, and it was grim reading. There had been progress, but it had been pitifully slow and some of it seemed due to more accurate data-gathering rather than real improvement. It was still possible that the government could meet its ambitious targets, but with statistics like the one that showed only two new houses had been completed in the Northern Territory in the last two years, quite a few fingers needed to be pulled out. The promise of an extra $90 million for pre- and post-natal healthcare might help, but the problems seemed to go deeper than money.

Some Aboriginal leaders thought that reinstating the *Racial Discrimination Act*, suspended by John Howard for his Northern Territory intervention, was vital; others argued that the intervention had already been heavily diluted. Wesley Aird urged Abbott to support Rudd, while Noel Pearson implored Rudd to cooperate with Abbott. The political debate among indigenous Australians was a good thing in itself, and a sign that they saw themselves as part of the wider society.

And there were other reasons to hope the despondency of the Howard years was at last starting to lift. The Rugby League that weekend was an unqualified success. The inspiration came from Preston Campbell, a Kamilaroi man from Tingha and the

brilliant fullback for the Titans, who had a vision of an indigenous team to showcase the Aboriginal and Torres Strait
Islander stars of the game. An enthusiastic and well-mounted
campaign brought the league, the media and the federal government on board. So Rudd and several of his ministers were at
Skilled Park on the Gold Coast to see Campbell's Indigenous
All Stars win a thriller against the NRL All Stars led by Kanga-
roos captain Darren Lockyer.

Rudd said it was all about indigenous pride, and he was
right. But all Australians could be proud that we were at last
back on track for true reconciliation. There was a lot to do, but
at least there was sincere goodwill and a measure of empathy
on both sides of politics. In this area at least we could report
genuine progress.

But on the more electorally important issue of the hospital
system, Abbott once again jumped in where Rudd was seem-
ingly too timid to tread. Immediately after being elected prime
minister he would, he said, appoint local boards to run the public hospitals in New South Wales and Queensland. This would
not solve the real problem, however, which was funding and the
blame game between the states and Canberra; Rudd would
have something to say about that in a week or two. It was a nice
piece of populism, appealing to those who thought everything
would be fixed if you could only get rid of the bureaucrats and
their red tape. But it wouldn't solve the problem, and we knew
it wouldn't because it had been tried before.

In the last, desperate days of the 2007 campaign, Abbott
tried this trick on the Mersey hospital in Tasmania, which was
miffed at being overlooked in that state's master plan to
restructure the system. The result was a complete breakdown
of the system, and it also pointed up the problems of local
management: every community would want the biggest and

best hospital and the empire-builders would compete to get their own high-tech facilities rather than share them on a rational basis. The result would be waste and duplication on an unprecedented scale.

The government dismissed Abbott's proposal as just another stunt, but once again it was an effective one. While Rudd dithered over the issue, Abbott promised action. This was certainly the line being pushed by Coalition supporters; Dennis Shanahan (who else?) crystallised it in the *Weekend Australian* by proclaiming that the ascension of a fellow conservative Catholic over that ultimate heretic, the liberal Catholic, had produced a stunning political turnaround; that the parliamentary week had been disastrous for the government and that 'all the hidden barnacles and seaweed on the dark side of the Rudd government's keel began to pull Labor down.' Well, things weren't quite as rosy as they had been at the end of the previous year, but it was hardly apocalypse now; Rudd was still flying a lot higher in the polls than the miracle man in lycra.

But the Labor hardheads did acknowledge Shanahan was right about one thing: the Coalition was now providing at least a semblance of unity. Abbott had unveiled his hospital policy in Malcolm Turnbull's own electorate, with every appearance of amity. And this meant that the media attention had now gone off the Opposition's nuttiness (always excepting Barnaby Joyce, of course) and was focused again on the government's problems. There was no doubt that Rudd was in real danger of losing the political initiative to Abbott.

It was time for the real Kevin Rudd to stand up. So where was he? For that matter, as some of the more sceptical punters were still asking, who was he?

> *If anyone had been paying serious attention to my puppet shows, I would have been sent to therapy very young.* —BOB BALABAN

★ 4.

THIS WAS A QUESTION even some of his closest colleagues were starting to toy with. Rudd had been St Kevin, the saviour who led them out of the political wilderness into the land of government perks and big white cars. But in 2010 he was no longer the political impregnable he had once seemed. The polls were still okay, but it couldn't be denied that the trend was now running against them, and if it continued at least some of the more marginal backbenchers would be in trouble. No one was talking about actual defeat; while Rudd's halo had undeniably slipped, he was still a long way ahead of Abbott on every measure that counted.

Except one: to the astonishment of just about everyone, Newspoll revealed that Labor had surrendered its lead on economic management and the Coalition was now considered the better bet by a margin of 45 to 40. Wayne Swan remarked with some justice that the government had become the victim of its own success; the track through the GFC had been so smooth and painless that the punters now took it for granted and were whingeing about the fact that the economy, and particularly interest rates, were now returning to normal. But most of his colleagues didn't believe it. After all, how could the Opposition's economic trinity of Abbott, Joe Hockey and *(shudder)* Barnaby Joyce possibly be considered better money managers than Rudd, Swan and Lindsay Tanner? It did not compute.

But the hardheads in the backrooms saw the poll as an indication of a deeper worry: that the government was in danger of committing the ultimate political crime – being seen by the voters to be Out Of Touch. Which brought us back to the question of Kevin Rudd, 2010. An easy answer to the question of why he was slipping was provided by Shanahan and Co. in the Murdoch press: Rudd was a chameleon, he stood for nothing, he was all spin and no action. But their more thoughtful colleague George Megalogenis had a rather different take: the problem was not too little action but too much. It was the old story of the duck swimming against the current: enormous amounts of frantic activity going on below the surface, but very little visible progress. Because Rudd was still trying to micro-manage everything himself, keeping huge numbers of balls in the air to no apparent purpose, the things that actually got completed tended to pass unnoticed.

The theory should have made sense to Rudd himself, who had told a *Q&A* audience that he had made about 600 firm undertakings before the last election and that almost all of them had either been implemented or were in the process of implementation. Well, hang on a minute. If this was the case then most of them had gone unnoticed, presumably because they had made no discernible difference to people's lives, so nobody cared. And some of the ones that had been noticed had not received universal applause; look no further than the ceiling insulation program, an ongoing saga to which we shall return. And then there were the ones that had not been announced before the last election but rather sprung on an unprepared and increasingly cynical electorate, like the rebate for free-to-air commercial television stations.

Communications minister Stephen Conroy, never the most admired of Rudd's team, had quietly, almost surreptitiously, announced that at their request he was knocking $250 million off their licence fees over the next couple of years, suggesting that the moguls and multinationals who controlled them were at one with the deserving poor. This was always going to sound unconvincing, especially to the moguls and multinationals who ran the rival Pay TV networks. They decided to fight back, and Tony Abbott, never one to miss out on a punch-up, joined them. He was immediately slapped down by the heavies from channels Seven, Nine and Ten; obviously he was hoping that the support of the others, particularly Rupert Murdoch, whose News Limited owns 39 per cent of Sky News, would outweigh the damage.

At first it seemed to be working. Murdoch's tabloid attack dogs became even shriller about the awfulness of Kevin Rudd while giving Abbott a very smooth run. But the strategy remained high risk; the Dirty Digger's favours are notoriously fickle and he does not like losers. If Abbott was seen to be unelectable, he would be cast aside like a burnt sausage at a barbecue.

It may have been significant that Abbott waited a fortnight before entering the fray and only did so after a private breakfast with Murdoch. A News Limited spokeslackey said that media policy was not discussed at the meeting, but the News Limited campaign against the rebate was already well under way by then. The spokeslackey made Murdoch's position clear: 'We've never asked the government – or oppositions before they become governments – for any money. But we don't like them giving money to our competitors with no strings attached.' Fair enough, but there were various favours Pay TV had asked for: access to major sporting events presently confined to free-to-air, and the ability to tender for the new Asia-Pacific TV network. The stakes were pretty high and each side started to accuse the other of attempting to duchess the relevant minister, Stephen Conroy. Conroy appeared to have been even-handed, accepting every invitation that was offered and indulging in as much hospitality as was available.

But Conroy's justifications for the $250-million handout were less than convincing. He cited the cost of changing to digital; but way back in 2000 the Howard government had kicked in $260 million for just that purpose. Then there was the expense of providing the statutory 55 per cent local content; but the commercial networks filled it up with quiz shows and so-called 'reality' TV, cheap as shit and half as wholesome. There was no suggestion that any of the $250 million might be spent on improving the quality. The *Australian* stepped up its campaign with a full-page attack on Conroy and all his works. The whole thing reeked of self-interest, indeed direct conflict of interest, but the government still failed to provide a convincing reply. Certainly commercial television, once described as a licence to print money, appeared an unlikely recipient for government largesse, especially at a time when spending was supposed to be undergoing stringent cuts across the board. Some commentators noted that the networks employed Rudd's old boss, former Queensland premier Wayne Goss, as their lobbyist, and this was the reason for their success. Pay TV seemed to have responded by enlisting Tony Abbott.

To make it clear that he was taking the job seriously, Abbott told a Tasmanian radio journalist that he was giving up sex for Lent. She appeared relieved, but her eyebrows raised when

Abbott went on to boast: 'The only one of the Ten Command-
ments I'm sure I haven't broken is the one about killing and
that's because I haven't had the opportunity.' Well that's something to be grateful for, but surely he'd remember if he'd made a
graven image? Well, maybe not. He had been forgetting quite
a few things of late, including who had won the 2007 election
and why. For Abbott had decided to open yet another front, this
time based around industrial relations. He was not, he insisted,
planning to bring back WorkChoices – golly gosh no, that was
dead and buried; but it hadn't been all bad, and he just wanted
to resurrect the good bits. The problem was that the bits he
nominated were precisely the ones the public had found most
smelly: unfair dismissals and individual contracts. Julie Bishop
helpfully added that something had to be done about penalty
rates too. Abbott promised that, of course, no worker would be
worse off, but the hoary assurance was drowned out by roars of
disbelief and outrage from both the government and the unions,
both of whom promised to campaign unremittingly against
Abbott and everything he stood for. They would have anyway,
but they could hardly believe their luck at being handed so
much ready-primed ammunition.

And they needed it. The government's other longtime
stand-by, climate change, seemed to have reached an impasse.
The true believers were still gung-ho, but for the general public
it had become a second-order issue – although, interestingly, a
Morgan poll still rated the environment as the top of the electoral hit parade, even ahead of the economy. Ross Garnaut
made a brief return to the airwaves to note that while there was
a lot wrong with Rudd's policy, it was at least vastly superior to
Abbott's, which was based on principles of centralised planning
he thought had disappeared with the fall of the Soviet Union.
While this was helpful, it was clear that, for the moment at

least, the issue was off the boil, and it would be an unacceptable risk to make it the centrepiece of an election campaign.

I was brooding over this thought when I stuck my head into a Labor fundraiser featuring Julia Gillard as guest of honour. We had a brief chat about election dates: 'I'll bet it's this year,' volunteered the deputy prime minister, very much the professional politician.

Gillard gave the assembled troops a fairly straightforward call-to-arms speech, which was received with more enthusiasm than it probably merited. There was also a certain amount of confidence; the local member, Justine Elliott, is now a minister and in 2007 widened her margin to 9 per cent. Technically, the seat of Richmond (NSW) is no longer marginal, and Gillard's visit was more about propping up Page, just down the road. Certainly she sent all the right signals, supremely competent and confident without being smug. Afterwards, the mob were engrossed by the news that Abbott had nearly been obliterated by a semi-trailer while making an injudicious stop at a known black spot to give a press conference on road safety. Opinion among the Labor faithful was sharply divided over whether the near miss had been a good thing or not.

The same doubts were also surfacing about Peter Garrett. Not that anyone at the gathering was prepared to declare him guilty; far from it. Any anger was directed squarely at his persecutors. For Abbott to have suggested that Garrett was somehow guilty of manslaughter because four people had died while installing insulation was, by any standards, over the top. After all, Abbott had been health minister for three years, and over that period he was warned constantly of the deficiencies of the public hospital system. If warnings from health officials were not enough, there were almost daily stories in the media of endless waits and intolerable crowding in emergency departments, women being forced to give birth in toilets, and patients being sent home to die because there was no room in the wards.

The minister was told that massive reforms and huge injections of money were needed; but Abbott's response, or that of his government, was to float the idea of a Commonwealth takeover and then abandon it, and to actually reduce Commonwealth funding as a proportion of the total. And people died – lots of them. So should Abbott have been sacked? Did he have blood on his hands? Did John Howard fail the people of Australia by failing to dismiss him? Well, yes, if you applied the same logic as Abbott was now seeking to apply to Peter Garrett.

There was no doubt that the insulation plan was a shemozzle, but the blame for the faulty installations and the deaths of employees goes directly to the installers who ignored established safety standards – the greedy bastards who sent young men into the ceiling without taking proper precautions or giving them sufficient training. For Abbott to blame Garrett was sheer opportunism. And in any case, for a member of John Howard's last government to have invoked the Westminster convention and the doctrine of ministerial responsibility at all was the sheerest hypocrisy.

But there was a feeling that Garrett was becoming too much of a diversion. Parliament and the media had talked of nothing else for a fortnight and there was no sign that the interest was waning. As a result the government was spending all its time in the trenches, and was unable to get its more positive messages out. Perhaps it was time for Rudd to cut his losses and inform Garrett that his resignation had been accepted, whether it was offered or not. This feeling no doubt intensified in the following week when the Opposition triumphantly announced that it had finally discovered the smoking gun.

A risk-assessment report from the well-respected (well, at least very expensive) legal firm of Minter Ellison warning of death, fire and other disasters if the home insulation scheme was implemented had been left languishing in the environment department for months; it had never been shown to the minister. Surely this was negligence, incompetence and downright maladministration at an unforgivable level. Well, that was certainly the first impression; but on closer inspection it turned out that the report was a Mickey Mouse affair, just one of a number of sources the department had received and its serious recommendations had already been acted on. And most importantly, in spite of what the Opposition and the media claimed, it had not warned of deaths, fires and other disasters at all.

Ironically the main warnings had been about the political problems associated with the scheme, and these had proved all too correct. As Rudd finally admitted, the program had been implemented ineffectively and a fair bit had gone wrong. He took personal responsibility and would go about setting things right. By the end of the week Garrett was off the hook, and was even being applauded in the party room. He lost responsibility for rejigging and reselling the scheme and the new relief package that went with it, which was obviously a smack on the wrist; but it was a pretty small bone to throw to the Opposition and media pack. Garrett remained a senior minister, a member of cabinet. By any normal standards he was still a winner. Rudd's own position was a little more complicated. If Garrett had been worth supporting and preserving throughout the whole brouhaha, why did he have to be demoted as soon as the heat was off? What devious spin was in operation here?

Well, none, actually, as Abbott, a veteran of the Howard years, should have known. The political reality is that ministers are sacked not because of negligence or incompetence but because they have become political embarrassments, when the cost of losing them becomes less than the cost of hanging on. Rudd did not believe Garrett had quite reached that point, so end of story – for now. But Garrett had been shown to be vulnerable. The Opposition would not give up the chase, and could have better luck next time.

★

If the Opposition was not yet ready to move on, the government was already galloping off in new directions. In her classic poem 'My Country,' Dorothea Mackellar notes that the Australia she loves is a land of contrasts – 'her beauty and her terror.' Politicians are seldom reluctant to extol the beauty, but in an election year the terror is often more useful. Rudd certainly found it so in the midst of the insulation uproar. His major statement on the subject was dismissed by some in the Opposition as merely a distraction from pink batts, but in fact the Opposition had been demanding this statement for quite a while and would have complained loudly had it been delayed.

The White Paper had been commissioned back in 2008, after the Mumbai attacks, so one could have expected it to be rather more substantial than it was; its essential message was that there was a fair bit of terrorism about, and that the government was against it. And so was the Opposition, insisted Tony Abbott in a rare moment of bipartisanship. But he was more against it than the government, so there.

Terrorism, we were warned portentously, had emerged as a permanent feature of Australia's security environment. Well, in an election year it would, wouldn't it? But then came the switcheroo: it was not just suicide bombers, and it was not just from overseas. Now the danger was far wider, and the perpetrators were likely to be among us – not just maddened jihadists, but the absolute scum of the earth, the vilest form of people on the planet, traders in human misery who should rot in hell – yes, people smugglers.

In a spectacular piece of political sleight of hand, Rudd conflated the threat to national security posed by organisations such as Al Qaeda and Jemaah Islamiyah with the challenge to border security posed by asylum seekers in boats. Yes, really; our top counter-intelligence agency, ASIO, was now to be unleashed against the wretched of the earth. ASIO, it should be recalled, was originally set up to investigate the espionage activities of foreign interests in Australia. Over the years it was expanded to deal with what was loosely described as internal subversion, which generally meant lefties. In intellectual circles in the '60s and '70s, to not have an ASIO file was to be seriously socially disadvantaged. But the essential criterion remained: ASIO dealt with perceived threats to the nation's security. It was expressly forbidden from investigating criminal activities or, if it came across any by accident, from passing the information on to the police forces.

Now Rudd broadened its powers dramatically. ASIO and the other spy agencies were to target people smugglers and their accomplices, both in Australia and overseas, with the aim of securing criminal convictions under new and draconian laws.

This would be time-consuming and expensive, so yet again the ASIO budget would be increased, as it had been every year since the organisation's formation in 1945. The political aim was to show, yet again, that Labor could be just as tough on border security as the Coalition, and to take the heat out of the accusation that the government had lost control of the influx of boat people. And who knows, it might even reduce the numbers a bit – although that would be an unexpected bonus. As long as the policy generated the right headlines, it would be seen as a success. And so far it had; even the *Australian*'s Greg Sheridan gave it an A plus, thus proving it could satisfy even the most devout paranoiac.

Now it was Abbott's turn to move on. He did so by targeting welfare with the hoary Tory cry demanding all but universal work for the dole for its recipients, including those with disabilities. This could possibly have been sold as a visionary and worthwhile move aimed at raising the underprivileged to independence and self-reliance, but unfortunately it was coupled with the insistence that all family payments remain universal and non-means-tested – taxpayers would continue to pay for millionaires to have babies. As usual the rich got the carrot while the poor got the stick. Abbott also signalled a return to the days of Sir Robert Menzies by signalling that he would seek to declare all Aboriginal settlements dry; among other things this would mean again suspending the *Racial Discrimination Act*, but for Abbott the outcome was more important than the principle. Once more, the Jesuits won.

Of more immediate significance was the Opposition's decision to again oppose the government's legislation to means test the private health insurance rebate. At least this was consistent; if we are going to subsidise the reproduction of the rich, the least we can do is kick in to keep them fit and healthy. The move gave the government its second double-dissolution trigger, but Abbott said he would be happy to fight an election over a broken government promise. It was true that Rudd had undertaken not to change the rebate in the lead-up to the 2007 poll, and because this was the only undertaking on which he had reneged, the effect was dramatic, even outstanding, like dog's balls.

On the other hand there was the argument that promises or not, bad policy is bad policy and should be changed. Much of the criticism of Rudd had been that he was being too cautious: he wasn't changing enough. His obsession with delivering exactly what had been foreshadowed in 2007 had been well received by the electorate, but taken to extremes it could itself be seen as good politics but bad policy. John Howard's appalling schools funding system, for instance, had been guaranteed for four years, and Julia Gillard continued to assure frustrated parents and teachers that it would remain in place. Abbott certainly had a point: Rudd had indeed broken a promise, and in doing so had tarnished his squeaky-clean, holier-than-thou persona. But he was only human; the previous week he had proved it by appearing on the commercial TV show *Good News Week* and actually doing quite well. In response Abbott announced that he had qualified for the Port Macquarie Iron Man contest. That was how a real man spent his leisure time. Rudd showed that he wasn't a complete wuss by announcing a fund to help Pacific Islanders become rugby stars. And then, totally unexpectedly, he undid most of the good work by going into a giant grovel. He had been advised by the apparatchiks surrounding him that the pink batts epic had not only diverted attention from the government's real achievements; it had become a damaging image in its own right. The Opposition was arguing that if Rudd's mob couldn't even run a home insulation scheme, how could they be trusted with the keys to the Treasury – and the ALP's internal polling showed it was starting to cut through. Obviously there had to be more positive action, but first a circuit-breaker was needed; even the anti-terrorism statement, which should have been the big story of the week, had to share the headlines with pink batts. So the idea was that Rudd should make a manly apology for the whole tedious affair; or, in the words of his advisers from the New South Wales right, eat a shit sandwich.

They probably meant that Rudd should say something direct and to the point: 'Look, the insulation scheme looked like a good idea at the time – what Gareth Evans once called "the streaker's defence" – but we didn't see the problems in time. I'll admit it, we stuffed up and we'll have to do better in future. I'm sorry for all the angst, now let's get back to work.' What neither they nor anyone else expected was that Rudd would emerge in sackcloth and ashes, wailing and gnashing his teeth, virtually beseeching the voters to punish him. 'Beat, me, whip me, flagellate me with bulls' pizzles,' he pleaded. 'It wasn't only the pink batts; everything my government has touched has turned to dust. We have proved unworthy, we are miserable sinners and deserve your loathing and contempt, which I fully expect to see manifested in the opinion polls next week.'

Those were not his exact words, but that was the impression left with a gobsmacked commentariat and electorate the next day. The best that could be said was that he had definitely put an end to the blame game; there would be no more buck-passing. From now on Kevin Michael Rudd, PM, was to blame for everything, and that was it. Appropriately he had chosen the Sabbath for his mea culpa, which gave the usual pundits a clear run into next week's media. The more religious among them might have noted (but inexplicably did not) that he had preceded it by making his own pilgrimage to Canossa; for years he had refused to appear with the talkback shockers of the lunar right, Alan Jones and Ray Hadley, or even take part in the ABC's almost painfully balanced *Insiders* program. Now he appeared like Henri IV before all three, praying for forgiveness and admittance. It must be said that the pontiffs of radio and television were kinder than Pope Gregory; they did not keep the suppliant waiting for three days barefoot in the snow.

They welcomed him with unconcealed relish and proceeded to give him the scourging he obviously craved. And that, the prime minister appeared to believe, should settle the matter. Okay, back to work.

But of course it wasn't as easy as that. The public seemed to greet the baring of Kevin Rudd's soul with the same mixture of disbelief and distaste they had shown at the baring of Tony Abbott's body. It was the kind of thing that should be done in private, if at all; and it certainly wasn't what one expected or wanted from a political leader. It smacked of a dreadful lack of self-belief. Rudd had been elected largely because he had appeared competent and confident, someone with the strength to protect and nurture his people, to take their troubles and concerns on his own broad (well, at least adequate) shoulders. But suddenly their saviour, the man who had led them through the GFC, was showing weakness, admitting failure. Was he, after all, unreliable? Might he even prove unsound?

Well, perhaps, but not quite yet. There is an old joke about the masochist and the sadist: the masochist says, 'Whip me, please whip me,' and the sadist smiles and says, 'No, I won't.' This is roughly what happened with the next Newspoll, which showed no real change in the government's standing: Tony Abbott was improving, but Rudd was still very much odds on. It was certainly not the whacking he had almost gleefully predicted. Perhaps that was still to come, but for the moment Rudd appeared to have survived both the pink batts and his own battiness. It left a strange aftertaste, the memory of which would undoubtedly linger on. And perhaps more importantly it got in the way of the great policy resurgence, which had started with the anti-terrorism statement and was set to continue into Labor's preferred territory of education and health.

One notable corollary from Rudd's weekend of penance

was that rather more attention was focused on Julia Gillard. She had been untouched by the pink batts controversy and, to the surprise of even her most fervent supporters, now stood as something of a rock of stability while others floundered around her. She had delivered Fair Work Australia, and although there were still problems around the edges, she was attending to them and the system was showing signs of bedding down. Gillard had also confounded her conservative critics with the My School website, which had also overcome initial glitches and was now generally accepted as a major reform. Indeed, Alan Jones, Labor's most assiduous and vitriolic detractor, had publicly endorsed her for the prime ministership, prompting an immediate round of leadership speculation from the more excitable Liberals. This was initially seen as mere mischief-making, but as Rudd's popularity began to slide, it took on something of a life of its own, albeit a very tenuous one. Rudd was the undisputed leader, but Gillard was increasingly seen as the one who made the actual deliveries. And now came the follow-through, the most concrete evidence to date that the education revolution was not just a slogan: the national schools curriculum.

This was the breakthrough that the industry had been waiting for. And to be fair, most of the industry greeted it with at least muted applause. The teachers, of course, called for more time to adapt to the changes and some state authorities bemoaned the passing of their own long-outdated programs. But almost all the new curriculum received a decent pass from almost all the stakeholders. The exception was the history syllabus. The cultural warriors of the right rose in righteous wrath at what they considered an utterly unjustified emphasis on indigenous history at the expense of their own beloved British tradition. Why, there was even a mention of Kevin

Rudd's Sorry Day included. Was the dreaded black-armband version making a return?

Such was the rage that some of the less stable members of the Opposition, including the education spokesman Christopher Pyne, threatened to can the whole curriculum and start again unless there was more waving of the Union Jack. A more rational approach came from Tim Hawkes, the headmaster of the ultra-conservative private Kings School, once an employer of none other than Alan Jones. Hawkes noted that just 39 of the 237 content areas in the history curriculum contained any reference to indigenous Australians – a bit over 16 per cent. Given that the Aboriginal history of Australia was at least 200 times as long as that of the white settlers, this hardly seemed excessive. By the end of the week there were indications that commonsense would prevail and that the long-awaited reform, with its guarantee of uniform national standards, would receive a fair trial.

But by the end of the week public attention was focused altogether elsewhere.

> **"** *Without the good will of manipulators and audience alike, puppets cannot sustain an illusion of life.* —MATTHEW ISAAC COHEN

 5.

AFTER TWO TORTURED and tortuous years, Kevin Rudd was finally ready to lay down his plan for the public hospitals. For the media and, one suspects, for the general public, it was the big one, the one they had been waiting for with increasing impatience, and it was a national sensation.

The Opposition promptly dismissed it on the grounds that it was a statement on hospitals, and not on the whole health system, taxation, the future of Australian society, life, the universe and everything. This was just bad politics – opposition for the sake of opposition – and it looked not only carping and negative but plain silly. Tony Abbott had himself once suggested the two themes: funded nationally, run locally. Although the funding wasn't quite national: the states would still pick up 40 per cent of the current tab. And the running wasn't quite local: the hospitals would be clumped in regional groups for administrative purposes.

But there was no denying that it was a bold, indeed revolutionary plan and one which demanded to be taken seriously. For the Opposition to pretend that it was just another distraction from pink batts was absurd. Almost as silly was the Sydney *Daily Telegraph*'s response of a hit list of 117 New South Wales hospitals allegedly under threat; they weren't. Rudd chose to see this as part of a conspiracy by power-hungry state bureaucrats – well, it takes one to know one. Perhaps his early years in Queensland were coming back to haunt him. But for whatever reason he made it clear that he was prepared for a battle with the states and that he would relish it.

So, apparently, would some of the premiers. Victoria's John Brumby replied that Rudd should simply hand over several buckets of money and piss off. The others, while slightly more conciliatory, started work on their own wish lists.

It remained possible that Rudd could win them over by his April deadline. Although the deal did not offer them what they really wanted – huge, untied sums of money – it did provide some relief from the ever-escalating cost of providing health services. They would lose, as a lump sum, 30 per cent of their revenue from the GST, but that was it; any future cost increases would be borne by the Commonwealth. But they would not be absolved of all responsibility, as would happen if the Feds took over the whole shebang by winning a referendum on the issue. The referendum, of course, was the ultimate threat, but it was one fraught with risks. If it were opposed by even some of the states, or by the Coalition as a whole, it would most likely fail, and then everyone would be back to square one. And for purely political reasons, if for no others, the Coalition would oppose it, just as they were threatening to oppose the current plan. The duty of an opposition, as Tony Abbott kept reminding the general public, was to oppose. Oh, and incidentally, where was the leader of the Opposition, the former health minister, the alternative prime minister, while all this was going on?

Well, lost, actually. Tony Abbott had mislaid himself in the course of a Boy's Own photo op somewhere west of Alice Springs. Yes, there he was, stranded in the trackless wilderness with nothing to drink but his aftershave and nothing to eat but the three journalists he had brought with him to record his epic expedition. A desperate effort to contact his press secretary proved futile. The dreadful ordeal lasted nearly five hours, ending barely in time for the late news. It made a fitting climax to a trip which had also seen Action Man Abbott eating a witchetty grub and hooning around on a quad bike. But don't think that there wasn't a serious purpose behind Tony's adventure tourism. As he put it himself, 'Serious leaders need to spend some time in remote Australia, particularly in remote indigenous Australia, to be aware of what's going on.' To prove his point he led the troops into a settlement called Hoppy's Camp, where he was photographed with two destitute Aboriginal men. Walter Shaw, president of the Tangentyere Council which covers the area, described the event thus: 'He barged into Hoppy's Camp with a huge media contingent and without an invitation or even the courtesy of telling people he was coming. This was rude and disrespectful.' Shaw also referred to 'comments not based on fact' and 'cheap shots in the media.'

Well, you can't have everything. And gee, the pics looked good.

So he had not been present in bodily form for the hospitals announcement, and when he finally re-emerged from the wilderness, he fell back on the line that if the government couldn't run a home insulation program, then it certainly couldn't run the health system. This was glib, but it missed the point; while he had been off on his excellent adventure the mood had changed. For the last thirty years governments, both state and federal, had been lamenting the decline of the hospitals network and predicting disaster unless someone, anyone, did something about it. And Rudd was at last doing something. His plan could certainly be analysed, criticised, vulgarised and bastardised, but it could not be shrugged off with a smart remark. And it was going to be perhaps the most important single issue in the coming election campaign. Abbott would have to do better.

But then, in another area altogether, he had a significant setback. The Coalition had been vigorously opposing the government's plans for changes to the Australian Building and Construction Commission (ABCC), the industrial police force John Howard had set up to bring the construction unions to heel. Rudd was honouring his promise to preserve the structure, but insisting on changes to make it rather more transparent and accountable, which Abbott and his workplace-relations spokesman, Eric Abetz, predictably described as a sell-out. Now Wal King, the president of the Australian Constructors Association, said that the big construction companies acknowledged that the government had a mandate for the changes and urged Abbott to let them pass in the Senate with only minor amendments. Heather Ridout of the Australian Industry Group agreed '1000 per cent.' Horrified at the idea of Rudd having a mandate for anything, Abetz threw up his hands and appealed to his long-time mates in the Australian Chamber of Commerce and Industry, who said of course there was no such thing. However the Master Builders Association said they accepted that there had been a mandate to end WorkChoices, although they'd really rather keep the ABCC as it was. Even the Liberals' traditional supporters were far from rock solid.

And in the *Weekend Australian* the invaluable George Megalogenis drew attention to another problem: while Abbott's leadership had seen a rise in the numbers who said they intended to vote for the Coalition, 20 per cent of those voters also said they preferred Rudd to Abbott as prime minister. That is, one in five of Abbott's own supporters didn't really want to see him in the Lodge. And the intended Coalition vote was still below that of 2007, when John Howard lost the election. At this stage the best that could be said for Abbott was that he was moving in the right direction but still had a long way to go in a fairly short time. This view was confirmed in the polling, which suggested that the events of the apparently tumultuous fortnight had not changed anything: the government was still comfortably in front, 53–47 on two-party preferred, and although Abbott had risen to 35 per cent as preferred prime minister, Rudd remained on 57. And most importantly, the first reaction to the hospital plan was massively positive: 79 per cent said they approved.

Rudd immediately set off on yet another Australian odyssey, this time to be photographed in hospitals and to talk to the premiers. Unfortunately when he was photographed with Kristina Keneally, the body language suggested they definitely weren't getting on and the prime minister was accused of snubbing the New South Wales premier. Both vigorously denied the charge – but they would, wouldn't they? Anna Bligh in Queensland seemed more compatible, but John Brumby in Victoria remained recalcitrant. In the west the only Liberal, Colin Barnett, was marginally less hostile and there was a somewhat surreal quality to the visits to the other states: both South Australia and Tasmania were facing elections by the end of the month and both were expected to be very tight indeed; next month Rudd could be renegotiating with a different premier altogether. Nonetheless, Rudd insisted it was a crusade to be fought and won – everything else, including the

Henry tax review, would have to wait. Under some pressure, Wayne Swan eventually promised the Henry review would be released before the May budget, but Rudd's priorities were well and truly set – so much so that he rushed out chapter two of his health plan, an extra 5000 GPs and sundry specialists as well. The health juggernaut was away and rolling.

The only thing that momentarily slowed it down was the visit of Indonesia's president, Susilo Bambang Yudhoyono, who, to the relief of sub-editors, prefers to be known as SBY. SBY was serious, frank and supremely constructive. And he identified the biggest problem between his country and ours: not the governments, but the people, who remained mutually suspicious and still felt vaguely threatened by each other. I could relate to this; only a few years ago I regarded Indonesia as a sort of post-colonial Javanese empire, dominated by doctrinaire Moslems and tenuously held together by a corrupt and expansionist military, an international loose cannon which could only be treated as potentially hostile to Australian interests. But in an astonishingly short time it has all changed: Indonesia is now emerging as a fully-fledged secular democracy, increasingly prosperous and confident of its place in the world, an unambiguously good neighbour. There is still work to be done but SBY, building on the foundation laid by the brilliant, if eccentric, Abdurrahman Wahid (Gus Dur), has helped to transform not just his country, but the entire region, for the better.

The politicians on both sides accepted and welcomed this, but the public in general had not caught up: a recent survey showed 54 per cent of Australians still regarded Indonesia as irresponsible in international relations, and we could assume the sentiment was returned in the archipelago. This outdated view must be corrected.

Educational and cultural exchanges and even tourism would help, but from the Australian side the most important step was to restore the teaching of Asian languages, and particularly Indonesian, in Australian schools and institutions. The program had thrived until it was inexplicably terminated under John Howard. Kevin Rudd had promised to reinstate it; SBY's visit should have encouraged him to start doing so at once. And for once he might even have had some spare time to fill: a more prestigious visitor, Barack Obama, announced with regret that he would not be able to slot in a visit to America's most trusted and reliable ally in March as promised. Like Rudd, he had a hard-to-sell health scheme and a rebellious Senate to deal with at home. This was a great disappointment to the numerous local tourist attractions which had put in optimistic, if hopeless, bids for a visit from the Obama family, but they could always try again, as the visit was rescheduled for June.

Fortunately Tony Abbott was, once again, available to fill the gap. Having alienated yet another voting group by confiding to the media that he felt 'a bit threatened' by homosexuals, Abbott made a Herculean effort to woo back the women's vote by gazumping Rudd's parental leave package – a relatively modest eighteen weeks at the minimum wage. To the amazement of everyone, not least his shadow cabinet and party room, Action Man declared the sky the limit. And promptly got shot down in flames for all the wrong reasons. You almost had to feel sorry for him.

In spite of what his apologists claimed, there was no doubt that unveiling the policy on International Women's Day was both rushed and rash. Abbott described it as 'visionary,' meaning, presumably, that it had come to him in a vision. He might have spent some months reconsidering his old 'over-my-dead-body' stance on paid maternity leave, but there was no sign that he took more than a few micro-seconds working out the details of his new one. This explained his remark about it being easier to apologise to his party room after the announcement rather than asking its permission beforehand. Had he done so, it is unlikely that it would have emerged in its present amorphous state.

The idea of six months' leave on full pay for everyone was appealing in its simplicity, but it hardly added up. Giving the cleaners $600 a week to have their babies while the executives got $3000 a week seemed, at the very least, a trifle unfair. Abbott obviously subscribed to the view articulated by a correspondent to the *Sydney Morning Herald* back in 2004: 'The rich need more money than the poor because they have greater expenses.' But considerations of equity aside, the scheme was vastly more generous than the government's and more than ten times as expensive, and the money had to come from somewhere. Abbott proposed a levy of 1.7 per cent on companies that earned more than $5 million a year – or perhaps that turned over more than $5 million a year, or perhaps that paid tax on more than $5 million a year, or perhaps that paid more than $5 million a year in tax: it was not immediately clear which. The levy would be, presumably, on the total taxable income of the companies, but again we were not quite sure. What we did know was that only the 3200 biggest companies in the country would be affected, and that they could all afford it. If not, they could always try putting a levy of their own on the salaries of the CEOs and directors – about 75 per cent might be appropriate.

The companies were appalled, of course; even Peter Anderson, the die-in-a-ditch Liberal chief executive of Abbott's normally rusted-on support base, the Australian Chamber of Commerce and Industry, said the policy didn't make sense, and Heather Ridout of the more moderate Australian Industry

Group said she couldn't believe Abbott was serious: the priority should be to lower company tax, not raise it.

And when not only the feminist groups but the Greens came out in support of Abbott, the economists crowed that this proved the idea was totally crazy: fairies in the bottom of the garden stuff aimed at undermining our prosperity and destroying our way of life. And then came the unkindest cut of all: Australia's greatest ever treasurer, the man we all thanked, loved and missed, the Liberal Party icon Peter Costello (as Abbott had called him at various times), wrote a piece for the latte-sippers' bible, the Fairfax press, calling it a silly policy and a betrayal of Liberal principles. Of course, he also rubbished Rudd's health reforms, but that was what he was supposed to do, not turn on the man with whose name he had been coupled so long and so intimately. *Et tu*, Peter? But why had his supposed friend, ally and mentor turned against him? Because he proposed to raise taxes.

And this was the real problem: not the substance of the policy, which was scarcely debated, but the fact that Abbott, as Opposition leader, was proposing a Big New Tax. This broke the first rule of opposition: never, ever admit that you might increase taxes in any way, let alone introduce a new one. Even in government it was a huge risk, as John Howard found out with the GST; in 1998, after a gigantic campaign funded by all the resources the taxpayers could provide, Howard barely scraped back with less than half of the popular vote. In opposition it was suicide; just ask John Hewson, or for that matter Mark Latham, who in 2004 refused to play the tabloids' silly game and guarantee no tax increases. This, declared the Murdoch press, made him unelectable.

There are times when good policy cannot be delivered without tax increases, even a new tax: if Kevin Rudd is serious about reforming the health and hospitals network to the standards the media are demanding, taxpayers – or some of them – will have to foot the bill. But you could bet he wasn't going to spell this out in an election year. He was not that crazy-brave. There was much to criticise in Abbott's policies: many were opportunistic and quite a few just plain bad. But in this case he was pilloried not for a matter of substance, but for having the courage to defy one of Australia's more mindless political shibboleths. In this context the reaction to his next action plan – to take control of the Murray–Darling Basin from the states – was comparatively subdued. The irrigators condemned it, the National Party condemned it, his own shadow minister Ian Macfarlane said it should only be contemplated as a last resort. But at least the ghost of Sir Robert Menzies did not rise from the tomb to lecture him on the sacred Liberal principle of states' rights.

And the polls continued to trickle his way. The two-party-preferred vote still predicted a comfortable Labor win and Rudd remained well ahead as preferred prime minister, but on a strictly personal level Abbott's popularity was rising while Rudd's was falling. This did not mean much unless and until it translated into voting intention, but it gave some point to Opposition taunts about Julia Gillard preparing to take over. Such taunts gave Abbott's colleagues something to talk about in Question Time apart from pink batts, a dead horse they continued to flog alongside a scarcely more energetic one, wastage in the school building stimulus package, aided by yet another *Australian* campaign.

Then Abbott, as was becoming his wont, lurched off in another direction entirely. As has been mentioned, the Opposition leader is a serious and sympathetic student of Aboriginal affairs, so it was somewhat surprising to hear him call for an end to Welcome to Country ceremonies. Abbott complained that the practice of white Australians beginning formal proceedings by acknowledging they are on Aboriginal land and indigenous Australians welcoming them to it was greatly overused and had become tokenistic – a mere ritual.

Well, yes, but so had the practice of playing the national anthem at sporting events or opening parliament with the Lord's Prayer. Such rituals were still important to some of the participants, and should cause no offence to anyone else. Indeed, the only person who claimed to be offended by Welcome to Country was the deeply sensitive Wilson Tuckey. Like most of what was condemned by the far right as political correctness, Welcome to Country was simply good manners. It was entirely appropriate in an inclusive and civil society. And as Abbott's old mate Noel Pearson pointed out, while practical reconciliation which delivered measurable results was vital to indigenous Australia, the symbolism remained important too. Abbott took the advice and backed off.

There was, after all, a more pressing distraction: two state elections. In Tasmania, the Greens were expected to regain the balance of power; with Labor pretty much on the nose and the Libs never particularly popular, the state's unique proportional system of voting meant that it had hung parliaments more often than not. But South Australia, in which the re-election of Mike Rann's Labor government had been expected to be a mere formality, had suddenly turned knife-edge. Abbott looked southwards in hope. And indeed the results in South Australia and Tasmania were hardly what Kevin Rudd would have chosen; a large swing against the Labor Party could never be called welcome news, even if the wash-up in South Australia at least was a lot better than the pessimists had feared.

In the end the damage was more psychological than psephological. In both states the issues were very much local rather than federal and Rudd himself took no real part in the campaigning – nor, for that matter, did Tony Abbott. There were no obvious federal implications, but the vision with which Rudd had come to power – wall-to-wall Labor governments indulging in the greatest exhibition of cooperative federalism ever seen in the country – was now well and truly laid to rest. A change of government in Tasmania might make the task of negotiating health reform more difficult, but in any case ending the blame game was already proving far harder than had been anticipated. In fact, having another Liberal premier to help carry the can for failure could even be a political plus.

And there were more immediate concerns. It took a while, but the whacking in the polls for which Kevin Rudd had been pleading finally arrived. It was a highly selective whacking: Rudd's satisfaction rating fell to just 48 per cent, with 41 per cent dissatisfied – his worst ever result. Comparable figures for Abbott were 47 and 38; this meant, said his breathless cheer squad, enthusiastically led by the *Australian*'s Dennis Shanahan, that Rudd's net satisfaction rating at plus seven was now lower than Abbott's at plus nine. Why, you could even say that Abbott was more popular than Rudd. Well, you could, but this would ignore the rest of the Newspoll, which pointed out that Labor was still on track for a comfortable election win and Rudd was still preferred prime minister by 55 per cent of voters, as opposed to 30 per cent for Abbott.

Rudd could now feel vindicated. Unfortunately, far from satisfying him, this taste of punishment seemed only to have stimulated his appetite. The masochist in him decided to wind up the parliamentary session by giving Abbott a giant free kick, and Abbott, declining to play the sadist, took it gleefully.

It is not clear which of the tactical geniuses infesting the prime minister's office thought that inviting Abbott to address parliament on the subject of health reform was a good idea. The reasoning, if it could be dignified as such, was presumably that health was Labor's strongest area, its preferred battleground, and this was where the government should concentrate the action. True, but health was also one policy area where Abbott could claim both experience and expertise. He had actually been health minister for three years, and while he mightn't have been a particularly brilliant one, he at least knew the tricks and traps of the portfolio. And more to the point, Abbott was a performance politician, one who revelled in the limelight. Inviting him to take the stage on his own terms was never going to be a good idea.

In the event it was a minor disaster for the government. Not only did Abbott deliver a melodramatic rant about the government's failures, he took the opportunity to neutralise one of its more damaging lines, the one about how he, as minister, had ripped a billion dollars out of the hospital system. In fact, as Abbott pointed out, on his watch the Commonwealth had increased its funding; the catch was that the states had increased theirs more. Thus the Commonwealth share fell from 50 per cent to 40 per cent. To make up the extra 10 per cent would have cost another billion dollars, which was budgeted in the forward estimates but ultimately not delivered. You could argue that it should have been spent, but you could hardly argue that it had been ripped out. Abbott sat down to roars of applause from his backbenchers and Rudd replied; he had a lot more substance than Abbott but a lot less theatricality. As a result the media generally judged him the loser on the day. But like a punch-drunk fighter he demanded more, and set up a full-scale debate on the subject with Abbott on national television.

This was just plain dumb. He was on a hiding to nothing. If he won, well, so what? He was expected to; that's why he was prime minister and Abbott wasn't. But if he lost, it became a public humiliation and would be treated as such by the voters. Rudd should have known all of this: winning the televised debate with John Howard in 2007 confirmed his own claim on the Lodge. At least one debate in the course of the formal campaign was both necessary and desirable. But to gratuitously throw in an extra one (or two) several months in advance was simply foolhardy. This man needed help – or at the very least a new group of advisers. The rumblings from the backbench, and even from the ministry, were becoming louder and more public. There was no suggestion of rebellion, but the cosy and well-disciplined consensus which had been such a feature of Rudd's first two years had suddenly started to look a little fragile.

As it turned out, he got away with the debate, or perhaps it would be truer to say that Abbott handed it to him on a plate. Proving that Rudd does not have a monopoly on callow and unworldly advisers, Abbott's team decided that there should be no new announcements; their leader should stick to his role as Opposition attack dog and simply tear into Kevin Rudd. But at the same time he was apparently warned to stay in control at all times; not to fall for any lures Rudd offered which might tempt him to go over the top. As a result Abbott gave away his own natural advantages – his flamboyance and spontaneity – and emerged as hesitant and petulant. His anti-Rudd cracks, like the one about the prime minister having experience as an anaesthetist during parliamentary debates, came over as juvenile sneers, which were marked down severely by the dreaded audience-monitoring worms reinstated by the commercial TV networks.

Abbott had already identified the worm as a filthy socialist crawler when it comprehensively rejected John Howard during the sole debate of 2007. Now it appeared that the loathing was mutual: Abbott had barely opened his mouth before the worm dived for cover and stayed there. However it rose for Rudd, who gave one of his best performances. He could not bring himself to abandon polly-waffle altogether; there were a couple of brief, eye-glazing periods. But on the whole he was communicative and unusually combative. And of course he had something to say: he was the Man with the Plan. Thus when he accused Abbott of constant negativity, the contrast was clear and com- pelling – so much so that when he concluded by asking Abbott to join him in a partnership to reform the system for the benefit of all Australians, it sounded half-way convincing. Abbott's demoniacal laughter in response marked the worm's low point of the debate.

The worm-manipulators gave Rudd a convincing win, 70–30. Using the old debating marking scale of 40 for matter, 40 for manner and 20 for method, I scored it as 80 to Rudd and 60 to Abbott, and the 60 was probably generous. Most other commentators put it closer; they pointed out, correctly, that just by agreeing to the debate Rudd had acknowledged Abbott as his political equal and the alternative prime minister. It would no longer be possible for Labor to treat him as some sort of aberration, a political joke perpetrated by a clueless and desperate Liberal Party – although the Opposition leader did continue to do what he could to help.

> *Some hypocrites and seeming mortified men, that*
> *held down their heads, were like the little images*
> *that they place in the very bowing of the vaults of*
> *churches, that look as if they held up the church,*
> *but are but puppets.* —WILLIAM LAUD

★ 6.

THE DEBATE TURNED OUT TO BE something of a returning point in more ways than one. Abbott's honeymoon came to an abrupt end both with his boosters in the media and with the punters. The polls turned dramatically; Labor surged back to a convincing lead on primaries and a huge twelve-point gap in two-party-preferred. Rudd's approval rating rose and Abbott's fell; Rudd was now preferred prime minister by a margin of thirty-two points. And most significantly Labor regained its lead over the Coalition in the vital area of economic management. It was a devastating verdict from the voters, but even before it had been received the pundits were voicing their concern. It was time, they felt, for the Opposition leader to throw the switch to serious. Poor Tony Abbott. As if life wasn't already confusing enough, now his backers wanted him to change his ways yet again.

The Mad Monk's career had always been a series of dilemmas and contradictions, and it must be admitted that he was yet to resolve even the most longstanding of them. Many decades after abandoning the seminary for the soapbox, Abbott remained torn between the sacred and the secular. His continuing doubts could be seen not only as anti-democratic, but almost as blasphemous; after all, the doctrine of the separation of church and state relies on the highest authority. Jesus said: 'Render unto Caesar that which is Caesar's and unto God that which is God's.' It could hardly be clearer. But Abbott still had trouble drawing the line and his political career continued to suffer as a result of his religious zeal.

The impasse also coloured his social attitudes, which tended to swing wildly between the ultra-conservative and the freewheeling liberal. In an interview on Channel 9's *60 Minutes*, he confessed that he felt 'threatened' by homosexuality before telling ABC TV that gays and lesbians 'challenge orthodox notions of the right order of things,' in tones that could have come straight out of Leviticus. But then a fortnight later he appeared at the Melbourne radio station JOY FM to insist that he was a great defender of gay rights and that he had lots of gay friends – well, at least three, and that wasn't even counting Alan Jones.

But this tergiversation was simple compared to what was demanded of him next: less action man and more policy wonk. It seemed so unfair. The Murdoch press, which was now urging him to settle into the role of serious and sober statesman, had previously been the greatest promoter of his natural, he-man approach to the job, contrasting it enthusiastically with that of the grey, spin-obsessed prime minister. His unbridled physicality was supposed to appeal hugely to the laid-back Australian voter, and especially to the women who might otherwise have been repelled by his Captain Catholic persona.

These same pundits had belatedly decided that policies were important after all, especially if Abbott was to have an outside chance of winning an election. Thus John Howard's former guru Arthur Sinodinos (the conservatives' Thomas Aquinas) advised Abbott to switch from the 'crazy-brave populist' to the 'Oxford-educated thinker,' and swap the Speedos and lycra for the suit and tie. Sinodinos refrained from suggesting that a spot of depilation might also help, but his message was unmistakable and reinforced by an editorial in the *Weekend Australian* on 27 March 2010: 'To win power he must craft a more positive image and show real leadership to a broader group of Australians.' Paul Kelly, even more pompous, pontificated in the same paper: 'The test is whether Abbott supplements his populist firebrand image with the assurance and reliability the public expects from a prime minister. He needs to reflect deeply on this multidimensional issue in its personality and policy aspects.' Well, that must have given the lad something to think about during the Port Macquarie triathlon on Sunday in which he was beaten by two hours by some bloke two years older than himself who just happened to be named Rudd.

But even before that event Abbott had made it clear that he was not going to stop doing what came naturally to him, and that certainly included hitting the beaches, the cycle paths and the jogging tracks. The defiant response must have come as a relief to charity groups like the one that auctioned a pair of Abbott's budgie smugglers on eBay. These raised more than $2000 after being worn on a mere two-kilometre swim, a terrific precedent; what might Abbott's jock strap bring in after next month's week-long Pollie Pedal? You could just about retire Barnaby Joyce's imaginary 'net debt gross public and private.'

And speaking of Barnaby Joyce, his demotion (and that's what it was, however vehemently his supporters denied it) did not solve all Abbott's problems. Getting him out of Finance was imperative, but finding a spot for what the leader described as his 'rare political talent' proved harder. After all, there are not many portfolios for which loud-mouthed ignorance is a prerequisite. He could not, of course, be sacked altogether; as the Nationals' Senate leader he held ex-officio shadow cabinet rank if he chose to exercise it. And having had a taste of it, he most definitely did. In the end Regional Development, Infrastructure and Water seemed the best fit: Joyce was now to be sent barnstorming around the countryside unleashing torrents of uninformed and probably inaccurate abuse, hopefully out of sight and sound of the national media. He would undoubtedly contradict Abbott's policy on water (Abbott favours a federal takeover of the Murray–Darling system while the Nationals and the irrigators do not) but this would likely prove less of a problem than his economic gaffes. And at least he would be out of the way.

The opportunity to shift him was provided by the unexpected resignation of Senator Nick Minchin, which posed its own problems. If Cardinal George Pell was Abbott's personal confessor in matters spiritual, then the sinister senator performed the same role in matters temporal; he was always the grey eminence lurking behind Abbott's leadership. No doubt he would continue to lurk, but his absence from cabinet meetings removed Abbott's most powerful ally. The moderates, led by Joe Hockey and Chris Pyne (who refers to his fellow crow-eater in terms that are unprintable even in the most enlightened media), were delighted. And what about the biggest moderate of all, Malcolm Turnbull? Suddenly Abbott's rejection of his well-publicised offer to return and take over the Finance portfolio looked less like prudent politics and more like a touch of funk.

Minchin would also be missed in his role as Opposition Senate leader, a position in which his unquestioned authority helped control the excesses of his Senate colleague Barnaby Joyce. His replacement, Eric Abetz, did not have the same clout. As his name implied, where Minchin took the lead, Eric merely abets.

After paying what was undoubtedly a sincere tribute to Minchin, Abbott found time between athletic engagements to deliver what he called, as John Howard did before him, a 'headland' speech. Just which headland he was commemorating was not entirely clear: Point Danger? Cape Tribulation? Hopeless Promontory? Okay, I made the last one up, but there was a touch of desperation about the address, which was perhaps understandable in the context of the latest polling. It was, Abbott's team emphasised, a headland speech – not a detailed announcement of policy. But even so, most were expecting more than another round of the pink batts and school buildings diatribe.

The only firm commitment that emerged was Abbott's promise to rein in government spending – to limit it, in fact, to 25 per cent of GDP. Given that revenue collection was well down as a result of the global financial crisis and was not anticipated to reach the 25 per cent mark for at least another two financial years, this amounted to a promise of truly massive cuts in government services or (but don't even whisper it) a large increase in taxes. The latter looked more likely, given that Abbott's only two serious commitments to date both involved large chunks of new spending: direct action on climate change meant hand-outs for the polluters and parental leave on full pay meant subsidies for the middle class. In the circumstances it was probably just as well for Abbott that most of the media buried the headland speech along with other trivia, such as the unstoppable Barnaby.

Determined to retrieve his reputation as a sound economic pundit, Joyce told one journalist: 'Well, if you are using it as a general stimulatory effect then you would suggest that the multiplier effect that would be attributable to, you know, the production of steel and the contractors that were involved would be similar to what is involved in delivering yet another modular unit, in some instances not even building it just transporting it.' *Phew*. And they said Kevin Rudd could waffle. Fortunately Joyce quickly reverted to form, asserting that he used the reports of the highly respected Productivity Commission as toilet paper. Abbott might have preferred the longer version.

★

As Kevin Rudd was cheerfully handing out miniature Easter eggs to the media, Abbott was busy preparing for his own Easter ritual – an attempted political resurrection as sole guest on the ABC's *Q&A*. It will be recalled that Rudd was generally thought to have done poorly in the same format. Abbott's team saw the occasion as his big opportunity to make a hit and gain revenge for the humiliation of the health debate. Abbott was low-key, polite – indeed, almost ingratiating to a fairly accepting audience – but not much was revealed. He admitted that he was not Jesus Christ, but added that Jesus Christ had never put up his hand to lead the parliamentary Liberal Party. And in response to questions about what 'the best man who ever lived' would have done about asylum seekers, Abbott pointed out that even Jesus had driven the money changers from the temple. It was a peculiar analogy; as Tony Jones pointed out, Jesus used a whip: was this to be seen as some kind of precedent? Abbott said he just meant that even Jesus didn't say yes to everybody, and nor would he. It was his most hairy-chested moment, and it was a clear signal that asylum seekers were well and truly back on the agenda.

In fact, the warning signs had been flashing for some time:

'The Australian government makes no apology for decid-
ing when certain people who come here as asylum seekers
are not legitimate asylum seekers.'—KEVIN RUDD, prime
minister

'We no longer determine who comes to this country and the
circumstances under which they come here. Mr Rudd has
given up that right, the right that should be part of being
a sovereign country.'—TONY ABBOTT, Opposition leader

'Our determination to stop the boats would be equal to
when we were last in government and John Howard did
stop the boats. We are not ruling anything out.'—SCOTT
MORRISON, Opposition spokesman

Remind you of anything? Yes, the rhetoric was hotting up in
much the same way as it did in the weeks before the 2001 election, the *Tampa* election, the children-overboard election, the
race election. Of course, Howard and his machine men vigorously denied that their dark victory had anything to do with
race, or at least not much. In fact it wasn't really about boat
people at all, it was about all sorts of other things like, um, er,
leadership. But the polling booths, each festooned with
Howard's implacable proclamation – 'We will decide who
comes to this country and the circumstances in which they
come' – told a different story.

It was a less-than-edifying episode in Australian history
and one which most of us had hoped would never be repeated.
But now Tony Abbott seemed to be heading in that unsavoury
direction. In the absence of any other clear policy from the
Opposition, he declared that boat people would be a major
issue at this year's poll.

Not the only issue, of course; let us not forget pink batts and school assembly halls. But since neither of those grave matters seemed to be capturing the imagination of the public – despite the very best efforts of the Murdoch press – we would have to rely on the asylum seekers.

And we knew they could be relied on. It is still not clear what causes the atavistic fear of boat people in the Australian psyche. It is demonstrably irrational; the vast majority of asylum seekers arrive by air, and in any case constitute less than 0.1 per cent of Australia's annual immigration. Yet somehow the boat people are supposed to represent a threat not only to our borders, but to our national security. Kevin Rudd had in fact unleashed the resources of ASIO upon these leaky vessels carrying insignificant numbers of the desperate and destitute into our waters.

So why the paranoia? My own theory is that it has to do with residual guilt. The original settlers arrived by boat, and from 1788 the trickle became a flood. Resistance was offered, but it was too little and too late: the Australian nation – in fact, a great many Australian nations – were overwhelmed, their way of life destroyed and their people killed, expelled from their lands and marginalised. It has happened before; just possibly it could happen again. Maybe, if we are not careful, the whirligig of time may yet bring about its revenges.

Whatever the cause, we knew from the 2001 experience that the issue was a hot one, and that it would not take much to revive it in an election year. Admittedly, Rudd had done his best to take at least some of the heat out of it. Where Howard and his ministers like the vampiric Philip Ruddock talked of asylum seekers as queue jumpers, illegals, disease carriers, drug pedlars, potential terrorists and eventually child murderers, not the sort of people you would want in this country unless they were permanently confined behind razor wire, Rudd urged compassion; his words and actions had been humane, with the closure of the hell-holes of Nauru and Manus Island, the abolition of the psychological torture of temporary protection visas and the relatively speedy processing of claims. But, unwilling to appear soft on border protection, he went over the top about people smugglers, 'the scum of the earth who should burn in hell forever.' They might not all have been in the mould of one of his heroes, the anti-Nazi people smuggler Dietrich Bonhoeffer, but they still provided a service the asylum seekers desired and used. To demonise them in such extravagant fashion was reminiscent of the way the Victorians used to persecute prostitutes while turning a sympathetic, or at least blind, eye to their clients.

As the quotation above demonstrates, Rudd and his advisers had clearly decided that he needed to counter Abbott's bloodthirsty rhetoric with some of his own.

There is a better way, and surprisingly it was eloquently articulated by a normally conservative commentator, Peter van Onselen, in the *Weekend Australian*. Van Onselen took the high ground in his appeal for calm: 'I find it disappointingly inconsistent that both of our political leaders, Rudd and Tony Abbott, wear their religion on their sleeves, yet neither of them practises the compassion that Christianity extols when it comes to boat people.' He acknowledged that at least some of Rudd's actions have been compassionate but accused Abbott of 'applying the rhetoric of former Labor powerbroker Graham Richardson to asylum seekers when he says that he will do whatever it takes to stop illegal boat arrivals.' Instead, he should pay more heed to the traditions of his Jesuit teachers, and embrace the concept of more 'compassionate conservatism.' After all, many asylum seekers who had been accepted had become successful small-business people, a core Liberal Party constituency. Van Onselen concluded: 'Australians shouldn't be afraid of boat people trying to come to our country. Our geographical position means that their numbers will always be small compared with refugee migration to other parts of the world. It's time our politicians started to lead public opinion on this issue instead of following it.'

Well, yes; but it would also be nice if Van Onselen could persuade some of his colleagues in the Murdoch press, not to mention their friends the shock-jocks, to stop beating the shit out of the issue. Then perhaps the pollies would feel able to calm down. As it was, Abbott at least had the grace to shift the goal posts a bit, or at least pretend to; he now wanted a broader debate about the level of immigration in general. For a long time this had been one of the few genuinely bipartisan areas within Australian politics; it was considered too sensitive and too dangerous for point-scoring. But now Abbott and his shadow minister Scott Morrison broke the pact.

The Intergenerational Report had predicted that Australia's population would reach 36 million by the year 2050; like all such long-term predictions the figure was little more than a guess, and Rudd let it pass through to the keeper while vaguely mentioning that he believed in a 'big Australia.' But Abbott hinted – and Morrison baldly stated – that it was too high. While Abbott was all in favour of Australian women breeding like crazy, he felt that immigration should be limited to suit the times. Morrison just felt that it should be reduced, although he seemed a little vague about the actual figures. He suggested that the current annual figure should be cut from 300,000 to 180,000; in fact, that real figure is already about 180,000. The 300,000 includes all the short-termers, ranging from holiday-makers to temporary workers. Since Morrison assured startled employer groups and tourism operators that these numbers would not be touched, it would appear that he planned to reduce the actual rate of immigration by two-thirds, a truly heroic slashing. Abbott quickly denied that Morrison meant anything of the kind, leaving what he did mean somewhat unclear. Both men, of course, insisted that their concerns had nothing whatsoever to do with the racial mix. Nonetheless, in the context of the pseudo-crisis about boat people, the debate had the potential to get very ugly.

Before Abbott and Morrison could take control of the debate, Rudd made his own move: without warning he froze the processing of asylum seekers from Afghanistan and Sri Lanka for six months and three months, respectively. It was hard not to agree with Abbott's description of the move as a quick pre-election fix – being seen to be doing something about an apparently intractable problem without actually achieving anything concrete. Rather than taking Peter van Onselen's counsel and showing leadership, Rudd had capitulated to the shock-jocks and to the scaremongers of the Opposition. Dennis Shanahan called it a populist response to a highly successful populist campaign waged by Abbott and Morrison; Van Onselen accused Abbott and Morrison of trying to rabble-rouse their way into government. The experts were appalled at the idea of placing people in detention for periods that could well be extended indefinitely with no real prospect of freedom at the end. This had been shown during the Howard years to be a near infallible formula for driving the victims insane.

There was little doubt that it was a cop-out, and one which was unlikely to provide the government with much relief. For a start, it was a broken election promise: Rudd's policy was that asylum seekers were to be fully processed within ninety days. Now the Afghans would have to wait twice that long before their first interview. The justification, if it could be so described, was that conditions had changed; the prospects of sending boat people home without a well-founded fear of being perse-cuted (the test for a genuine refugee) were now brighter. But this assessment was highly dubious. Sri Lanka was certainly more stable; but then, the most ruthless dictatorships often are. The stability did not mean that the government would be any less brutal to what it saw as rebel Tamils, especially those who had attempted to flee its shores. And Afghanistan, of course, remained a bloody mess, as it always had been and probably always will be.

Manuel Jordão, a senior official of the United Nations High Commissioner for Refugees, may well have been right when he said that people smuggling, with the introduction of spotter's fees and cut-price fares, was out of control. Rudd's move did nothing to bring it under control; at best it might buy him a little time. Given that his opponents were constantly accusing him of procrastination, this might not be the shrewdest of moves. So he followed it almost immediately with something decisive: the announcement that the Curtin detention centre would be re-opened to take the overflow of boat people. Curtin, near the Kimberley township of Derby, was the most remote and feared of all the mainland camps during the Howard era, and conservative commentators such as Dennis Shanahan, who had previously defended its facilities as being those of a holiday resort, now gleefully described it as a hell-hole. Rudd had decided that he could no longer afford to be Mr Nice Guy on the issue, and the timing was interesting: Rudd's apparent retreat from principle and compassion came almost immediately after Malcolm Turnbull announced (on Twitter, of all places) that he had decided to leave politics altogether.

Rudd, like many other reasonable Australians on both sides

of politics, might have still cherished the hope that the Libs would see sense, end the Abbott experiment and move back towards the centre-ground of politics, and that the process might entail the resurrection of Turnbull as leader. Turnbull himself might have harboured a similar fantasy – until, that is, his offer to return to the front bench as Abbott's spokesman on finance was rejected with something like contempt. Apparently Turnbull, generally acknowledged to be one of the smartest and most energetic figures on the floor of parliament – and certainly well ahead of anyone else on the conservative side – was not considered worthy of even that menial role. Obviously his continuing support for an ETS didn't help, but wasn't the Liberal Party supposed to be a broad church? He was to be cast into the political dustbin alongside Barnaby Joyce. This would have been a major humiliation to anyone with an element of self-regard; for Turnbull, whose self-regard borders on egomania, it was simply intolerable. He announced that he would serve out his term and then return to the private sector, perhaps to enter the field of sustainable energy production. On climate change, at least, he had not given up the fight.

His decision was greeted with much lamentation in the media: commentators recalled the fact that he had been destroyed for sticking to his principles, while glossing over the fact that they had been among the principal agents of his destruction. He was urged to rethink his resignation by many of the voters of Wentworth, and then by some Liberal apparatchiks who belatedly realised that Turnbull's personal following might well be the only thing preventing the seat from going to Labor next time around. But for the time being he remained firm, and the prospect of a moderate revival in the Opposition ranks more or less vanished for want of a credible figurehead around which to group. It may have been this realisation that persuaded Rudd there was no real alternative to a hard (or at least harder) line when it came to asylum seekers.

The scene had changed in other ways too – or rather, it had not changed in quite the way it was expected to. The wash-up from the two state elections left Labor in power in both. In South Australia, Mike Rann lost the popular vote but Labor's concentration on the marginal seats left him with a workable majority in parliament. In Tasmania the Hare–Clark system had, as forecast, delivered a hung parliament of ten Labor, ten Liberal and five Green. The Labor premier, David Bartlett, true to his word, had recommended that governor Peter Underwood commission the Liberal leader Peter Hodgman to form a government; the Libs had polled more votes than Labor, and this was seen as the tie-breaker. But Underwood was unconvinced: his own sources told him that the Greens were more likely to provide stability for a Labor administration than for a conservative one, and this was eventually confirmed by the Greens leader, Nick McKim. So Underwood followed convention and left the existing government in place; Bartlett had greatness thrust back upon him and started haggling with McKim. So Labor dominance across the map of Australia was unchanged: Western Australia's Colin Barnett remained the sole Liberal premier or chief minister, a fact Rudd hoped would be an advantage in his next big battle: hospital reform.

Fie, fie! you counterfeit, you puppet, you!
—William Shakespeare

★ 7.

While Tony Abbott had been bicycling his way through some freezing cold marginal electorates in the Pollie Pedal, Rudd with his health minister, Nicola Roxon, had taken to the sky, dropping in on every regional hospital within range of an airstrip. He would much rather have been somewhere else; in Washington, to be precise, which was where Barack Obama was hosting forty-seven world leaders at a conference to discuss one of Rudd's favourite issues: nuclear disarmament and safeguards. He had planned to attend, but had been dissuaded; while the nickname Kevin 747 had gone into abeyance, his enemies were still pushing the line that he spent too much time overseas when he should be looking after Australians at home. The more balanced commentators said that the Washington conference was a genuinely important international event and that Rudd, as head of government of one of the world's largest suppliers of uranium, had both a right and a duty to attend. But the spin doctors said no: hospital reform had become crucial to the government's re-election chances, and Rudd could not afford to take his eye off it, even for a couple of days. For good measure, they insisted that he also cancel plans for a visit to the Shanghai Expo. Rudd reluctantly gave way and hit the road – or rather, the airways, but domestic routes only.

The safari was a truly epic one. Although the main concentration was on New South Wales and Queensland, few local papers missed out on a photo of Rudd sitting on the bed of some suffering patient, who patiently suffered the intrusion in exchange for a moment of fame. This, of course, was the point of the exercise. Rudd said later that he had learned an enormous amount about hospitals, and indeed he could hardly do otherwise. But more importantly, he had shown that he cared; he was there on the ground, visiting the sick and comforting the afflicted. And he frequently had a spot of good news to announce as well. The result was hugely favourable coverage from the local media. The national media could unearth as many critics of the scheme as they liked; people saw the prime minister in their local paper and heard him on their local radio and overwhelmingly they liked him.

They certainly liked him a lot more than they liked their bumbling premiers, and that was what really counted, because the premiers, however unpopular, were steadily bumbling their way to a position that would make an agreement on health impossible and could trigger the ultimate threat of a referendum. Interestingly, the most intransigent was not the Liberal Barnett; he was, of course, opposed to the idea of any takeover by the Labor Feds as a matter of principle, but this could be dealt with. The real stumbling block was Victoria's John Brumby. Brumby already had form: it had been his parochial bloody-mindedness which had stalled the process of water reform in the Murray–Darling Basin, and now he was lining up for a repeat performance on health. He had his own formula for hospital reform: Rudd should simply give him a gigantic bucket of money and then piss off. As the days went by, he refined this a little: Rudd should give every state a bucket of money and then piss off.

The core principle remained. The Commonwealth might collect the GST, but that was its only role. The GST belonged to the states, and the idea of taking 30 per cent of it away so the Commonwealth could spend it (and a lot more) on increasing its share of hospital funding to 60 per cent was not on. The idea was unthinkable, a bolt from the blue. It was pointed out that Rudd had in fact canvassed it in his 2007 policy speech, a document in which one imagined Brumby might take a passing interest. No, he hadn't seen it. As far as he was concerned, it was his GST and they were his hospitals and Canberra could get its grubby hands off them. Just give me the money – 50 per cent of the funding, and after that it's business as usual. In other words, the Commonwealth should just hand over some $32 billion (which is what it would cost over the four years of the agreement) for no return whatsoever – no reforms, no guarantees of improvement, no timetables, no benchmarks, no nothing. Brumby justified his belligerence with the claim that Victoria's hospitals were the best in Australia and any attempt to impose national standards could only make them worse. Analysis showed that this statement, too, was not altogether true. Victoria's hospitals were ahead of the pack in some performance areas and behind in others. But the man even his fellow Labor premiers called 'The Terrorist' was not interested in that kind of argument. Like he said, Victoria was his state, and he could break it if he wanted to.

It was tempting to dismiss all this as bumptious bravado; a spot of Canberra-bashing in the lead-up to the state election Brumby was facing later in the year. Apart from Barnett, only Kristina Keneally in New South Wales had given Brumby any real support, and that waned rapidly as it became obvious that although some of the health-provider groups had their criticisms of the Rudd plan, and that some were driven by real concern as well as by self-interest, the voters remained firmly on side. There were some suggestions that the final decision should be postponed, but for Rudd, running over a year late, any further delay was unacceptable. The political timetable was already desperately tight; if the talks did break down and he was forced to take up the referendum threat, there would barely be time to get the legislation through parliament before the election. Indeed, there was no guarantee that he could get the legislation through the Senate at all. Most commentators assumed that Abbott would have to allow it; after all, by blocking it he would effectively be denying the voters a choice on health reform, and this could look very bad. But Brumby was apparently willing to be seen as the man who derailed health reform, and was willing to risk the wrath of his own voters. As the troops assembled in Canberra on 18 April, there were more possible outcomes than in your average Melbourne Cup.

Rudd and his health minister, Nicola Roxon, were somewhat pessimistic about the outcome. While Rudd had little doubt that his marathon trek through the provinces had been a popular success, he noted that Kristina Keneally had firmed up her opposition to surrendering the GST, and this meant that she, along with Brumby and Barnett, were now lining up to say that it was a matter of high principle, irrevocable and non-negotiable. Three of the six premiers were, they said, prepared for a fight to the death. However, experience over the years had proved to Canberra that every premier has a price; it's only a matter of finding out what it is. So, having loaded several wheelbarrows full of money, Rudd and Roxon went to work. It took two days of hard yakka: Rudd first softened the opposition up with an extraordinarily tedious PowerPoint presentation of his scheme, and then started doling out he goodies. First Keneally collapsed; then she helped Rudd gang-tackle Brumby. Suddenly the sacred principle of the GST was not quite so inviolable, at least not when $5 billion-plus was on the table.

Rudd seemed happy to go on ladling the stuff out indefinitely but Barnett, breaking the habit of a lifetime, said it was no good; he was not in it for the money, and in any case Rudd would have to give him his share of it if he wanted to avoid an electoral debacle in the west. Barnett was following a good historical precedent: at the time of federation, Western Australia refused to sign up with the other states, holding out until the sandgropers were offered the ultimate bribe: a railway from Kalgoorlie to Port Augusta, to be built at the Commonwealth's expense. Rudd was confident that something similar could eventually be arranged; the wheelbarrows were not quite empty – nor should they have been. Australia, believe it or not, spends a smaller proportion of its national income on health than does the United States – less, in fact, than any other industrialised countries except Mexico, South Korea and Poland. Rudd's apparent largesse was just playing catch-up. So it was hardly surprising when his office let it be known that he was prepared to spend even more to secure an agreement.

It should be noted that Brumby's price was not just the moolah, vital as that was. He had also insisted that the states retain a measure of control in the administration of the hospital funding, and Rudd had acquiesced. In many ways this was a surprising demand because the whole idea was to relieve the states of the responsibility, and therefore of the blame. The concession meant that Brumby's constituents, along with those of all the other premiers and chief ministers, could still point the finger at him if they did not see the improvements they had been promised. Rudd had volunteered to carry the can for all of them; knocking the offer back seemed positively perverse. The belief in Canberra was that since the Commonwealth would be setting the basic conditions under which the funding would be administered, it would have effective control anyway, and eventually the remaining state influence would wither away. But even leaving Barnett aside, which Rudd did in his media victory tour, it was less than a total triumph. And it cost Rudd one of his most important allies. Professor David Pennington, generally acknowledged as the country's foremost authority on public health, initially endorsed the Council of Australian Governments' (COAG) agreement, but on a closer reading he declared it would make little, if any difference – the meeting had 'degenerated into arguments about money and control, not about healthcare reform.'

Other health professionals also criticised the package, often for self-interested reasons, and Abbott, pausing between the Pollie Pedal and the Bondi Blue Water Challenge, gave no immediate guarantee that he would support it; Labor strategists could only salivate at the prospect of the Coalition and Steve Fielding (who had imperiously demanded a full personal briefing from the prime minister as the price of his vote) blocking their reform in the Senate. That kind of political bonus would make the whole exercise worthwhile.

There was no doubt that on balance the hospital plan remained a political plus. Rudd was acting where his predecessors had feared to tread, and he finally had a centrepiece for his election-year campaign. And there had been another useful, if unforseen outcome: even the staunchest conservatives were now having second thoughts about the wisdom of our founding fathers in reserving so much power for the states.

Historically, this retention was hardly surprising, since those same founding fathers were all colonial politicians dependent on the support of their local constituencies, who were just as parochial as today's state-of-origin crowds. So when it came to drawing up plans for federation, the key question was not how much power the Commonwealth government would need to function effectively, but how much the states could retain for their own administrations. Defence and what was then called external affairs had to be ceded to the central government, but that hardly mattered because Australia's foreign interests were seen to be identical with those of Great Britain, so Whitehall was calling the shots anyway. The free-traders won a few concessions, which gave the Commonwealth the customs service and limited jurisdiction over shipping and railways, but that was about it; the states were left with health, education, law and order, most transport, ports and harbours and anything else that wasn't specifically handed over. And of course they had their own parliaments and their own law courts – just about all the apparatus of a real nation except a standing army, although there have been times when their police forces seemed almost to be filling that role.

So just what are these bloated and self-important entities, anyway? They are the former colonies whose territories were originally determined by bored British civil servants drawing lines on inaccurate maps of places that they had never seen. For the most part the boundaries are purely arbitrary; even in the rare cases when they are based on geography (the Tweed and Murray rivers), they have absolutely nothing to do with the economies of the regions, let alone the popular culture. The anomalies are both obvious and absurd: the people of far western New South Wales, for instance, have adopted the time zone of South Australia, and the ongoing disputes over daylight saving meant businesses on either side of the Queensland–New South Wales border have made similarly confusing adjustments in summer. It is obvious that the residents of, say, Tweed Heads have more in common with those of the Gold Coast than with those of distant Broken Hill, but the state lines recognise no such reality. And until the 1950s passengers between Australia's two largest cities, Sydney and Melbourne, had to change trains at Albury because each of the states had its own jealously guarded railway gauge.

The situation is beyond ridiculous and the High Court – a Commonwealth institution – has recognised the fact by slowly but consistently eroding state powers as far as the constitution can be stretched. This move towards centralism has been resisted by the conservatives, who bleat about state's rights; but they are also the first and loudest to complain about the waste, duplication and inefficiencies the system generates. And indeed it was the conservatives who were the most consistent advocates of a national schools curriculum, even if some of them didn't like the version that emerged. During the Howard years there was an attempt to wrest water management from the states, and Tony Abbott, as health minister, canvassed the idea of a total Commonwealth takeover of the hospital system. So with both sides of politics moving in the same direction, perhaps it is time for another look at the can of worms that is our federal system.

Certainly the public is ready for it; study after study has found an overwhelming view that we are over-governed, with the states considered the least efficient and most dispensable of the three spheres. The replacement of both states and local councils by a system of regional governments based on commonality of interest and need was first proposed forty years ago by Gough Whitlam; and, incredibly, John Howard announced the week after the 2010 COAG meeting that it was the one subject on which he and Gough Whitlam agreed. The man who once described himself as the most conservative leader the Liberals had ever had said that if we were redesigning the federation from scratch, you would indeed have regions rather than states. Bob Hawke, who was on the same platform, agreed, but with one reservation: keep the state boundaries for Sheffield Shield cricket and state-of-origin football. Of course, getting rid of the states requires a huge change to the constitution, which many if not all of the premiers would resist. The obstacles to actually implementing such a policy remain immense, but perhaps – just perhaps – it is finally time.

Rudd's approach to hospital reform at COAG may have resulted in less than total, overwhelming victory; but it did indicate a somewhat less conciliatory strategy as the election, one way or another, got closer. Quite suddenly our beloved leader was no longer the caring, humane Christian, friend of the homeless, chronicler of economic history and dumb animals, star of TV, Facebook and Twitter, but a calculating, ruthless, whatever-it-takes politician, a veritable born again Richo. Well, probably not; Rudd is a far more complex and complete specimen of humanity than the notorious numbers man. But there were moments in the last weeks of April 2010 when the similarities were more apparent than the differences.

Rudd retreated to Tasmania while his perpetual clean-up man, Greg Combet, was sent out with the bad news of the inevitable, final demise of the home insulation program; the remaining money would be needed to repair any damage resulting from the roll-out. This announcement prompted cries of betrayal from the genuine insulators who had stocked up in anticipation of its return and Tony Abbott triumphantly proclaimed that the decision to set up the scheme had been 'the worst government initiative in Australian history.' As I reminded his predecessor Malcolm Turnbull when he used the same line some weeks earlier on *Q&A*, this was a bit over-the-top for those of us who recalled the decisions to join the American wars in Vietnam and Iraq; they had resulted in rather more deaths and disasters without even the benefit of leaving a million roofs insulated.

Another junior minister, Kate Ellis, was given the job of unobtrusively breaking another promise: only thirty-eight of the 260 childcare centres aimed at ending 'the double drop-off' would actually be built; apparently other places were available and the double drop-off was no longer important. Asylum-seeker policy had already been reversed. A task force was examining the Building the Education Revolution program and the auditors were sent in on the Green Loans scheme. And to cap it off, the government pulled the plug on any pro-posal for a bill of rights for Australia, a move welcomed by the autocrats of News Limited, who know all about human rights and don't want any unelected judges interfering with their monopoly.

This orgy of recantation by the government was euphemis-tically described as 'clearing the decks.' Fortuitously, much of it coincided with the revelation that a football club had overpaid some of its players, a news event of such magnitude that it swamped the media for the rest of the week and seemed likely to perform the same salutary function until the leaking of Ken Henry's tax review and the beginning of the budget. Inter-estingly the Melbourne Storm, the club responsible for this earth-shattering crime against civilisation, was wholly owned by News Limited, whose chief executive John Hartigan indig-nantly denied any knowledge or responsibility. This lame and self-serving excuse was apparently quite acceptable, at least to the News Limited publications. The *Australian* was considered unlikely to demand his resignation with quite the fervour with which it had pursued Peter Garrett over the pink batts affair.

Similarly, it appeared that Rudd would initially get away with his massive backdowns. Up to this point he had been almost obsessive about honouring his election commitments, determined not to fall back on the Howardian formula of 'non-core promises' even when there was good reason for doing so. The only real exception had been the private health-insurance subsidy, and even then Rudd's proposal was only to means-test this absurd measure rather than abolish it altogether, as he should have. But the new battle plan involved a relentless determination to kill off difficult or embarrassing loose ends in what was clearly the lead-up to a no-holds-barred election campaign.

We were still getting glimpses of the old Kevin 07, the avuncular figure who had won the nation's trust a mere three years earlier. Dr Jekyll had not yet morphed irrevocably into Mr Hyde. But it was a safe bet that in the weeks ahead we would see rather less of Mr Nice Guy.

Then came the big one: the emissions trading scheme, the focus of so much energy and angst, was taken off the agenda, at least until the end of 2012. The greatest political, environmental, social, economic and moral challenge of our generation, the absolute necessity of urgent action, the issue too vital to delay, the one where prevarication meant more risk and more expense, the watershed between the politics of the future and the politics of the past – well, it was to be quietly despatched to the back burner.

The decision came as both a disappointment and a surprise, given that only the week before Rudd had given an interview in which he said that the great moral challenge was undiminished and that the government would persevere with its efforts to get an ETS into place. 'It's very clear cut that whether climate change is topical or not, whether it is popular or not, the reality of it does not disappear,' he insisted. But he hinted that perhaps it was no longer a case of crash through or crash. Much would depend on the make-up of the Senate after the election, and in any case, 'national action in the absence of global action doesn't add up to a row of beans.' The implication that Australia should not take the lead but should instead wait for the rest of the world was uncomfortably reminiscent of the old Opposition line which Rudd and his colleagues had persistently derided; but now it was to be used as an excuse for junking the long-standing commitment. That, and the awful obstructionist Senate, of course.

But if the Senate was really the problem, why not go straight to a double-dissolution election, which, assuming Rudd won, would almost certainly give him the numbers to pass the ETS at a joint sitting of parliament? This course of action seemed not only logical but probable, especially when the word was passed around the ALP network from head office that it was time to put on the roller skates; the campaign could begin very shortly after the budget. Some excitable foot soldiers took this to confirm Farmer's forecast of 4 July, although more mature heads realised that this would involve curtailing the budget sittings of parliament and might smack of panic; if there was to be a double dissolution, and this was still a matter of con-siderable debate, then August was a more likely bet. When Penny Wong took to the airwaves to justify the ETS decision, she threw more cold water on the idea by repeating Rudd's mantra that the public generally expected governments to serve out their full term.

The real argument against rushing to the polls was the ETS itself: as its withdrawal made very clear, the politics had changed. The voters, once red-hot for action, had cooled off; the relentless campaign waged by the sceptics and the vested interests in the polluting industries had had an effect, although they had not had it all their own way; a report from the respected Grattan Institute pointed out that the real cost to most industries of implementing the kind of scheme Rudd had foreshadowed would not be anything like as drastic as had been claimed. The coal, alumina and natural-gas people, all of whom had been crying poor and threatening to move offshore, would hardly notice it in the context of their other expenses. Steel and cement might hurt a little, but a simple tariff could keep them competitive. And as Rudd was proposing to hand them all zillions in compensation to give them time to adjust, their cries of doom and gloom could and should be dismissed as naked avarice. But the polls showed that the punters were steadily going sour on the idea of actually having to pay to reduce emissions. Electricity prices were rising anyway, and the drought had broken; perhaps traditional Australian apathy was the way to go. Something might turn up, and if it didn't, we'd just have to muddle through.

This was precisely the attitude Rudd had criticised successive Liberal leaders for exploiting. He had repeatedly dismissed the proposal that Australia should wait to see what the rest of the world did as political cowardice. He had proclaimed from every political pulpit in the land that any delay in acting was unacceptable, a sacrifice of the future of our children and grandchildren, and that caution was an unacceptable risk that would prove horribly expensive. And for a while the voters believed him; a great many of them still did. They may have flinched at the idea of putting their money where their mouths were, but they had been prepared to do so in the past and, unless Rudd and his ministers had lost all self-belief, could be talked around again. Obviously Copenhagen had been a disappointment and Abbott's simplistic scare campaign about a great big new tax on everything had had some effect. But to back down in the face of Abbott's primitivism really was an act of cowardice – indeed, of abject surrender.

I once defined a politician thus: a politician is someone who genuinely and sincerely believes that the worst thing that could happen to the country is for him or her to lose his or her seat. Now Rudd, as befitted an international statesman, had significantly upped the ante: he felt that for Abbott to displace him at the Lodge would bring doom not only to the country, but to the whole world. He must honestly and sincerely have believed that his defeat would be a worse disaster than the most terrible predictions for the future of the planet. The true believers were, of course, devastated; they were still reeling from the assault on asylum seekers, which was barely forgivable. Now Rudd was altogether ripping the rug out from under them.

Labor strategists obviously calculated that in electoral terms it didn't really matter; the true believers had nowhere else to go. They were not going to switch to Abbott, whose position wavered between cynical scepticism and outright denial. And if they lodged a protest vote with the Greens, their preferences would ensure that it came back to Labor anyway. True, the switch would improve the Greens' chances in the key inner-city seats, many of which were held by ministers. Lindsay Tanner (Melbourne), Anthony Albanese (Grayndler) and Tanya Plibersek (Sydney) would all have been disturbed by the decision, had they been informed of it; apparently the deliberations were confined to a very small inner group and the rest read about in the papers, which didn't improve morale. And the jitters became more general when the backdown was also attacked by industry leaders. Brad Page, chief executive of the Energy Supply Association of Australia, was scathing: 'Now neither side of politics has a tenable policy – the consequences will be quite dire if people can't make investment decisions.' The Investment Group on Climate Change said the decision would mean less investment in renewables and the Santos oil and gas company said it would stall lower-emitting gas projects. About the only good news was that coming rises in the price of electricity would be less than forecast; but since the rises would still be substantial, this was hardly calculated to get the voters dancing in the streets.

Rudd decided to make the best of an irretrievable situation by re-announcing what he now described as 'the biggest ever investment in renewable energy.' There were two problems here. First, almost all the program was already on the table; there was no new bonanza to compensate for the deferral of the ETS. And in any case, Rudd and Wong had repeatedly insisted that the only effective way to tackle climate change was to put a price on carbon, a policy they had now abandoned for at least three years – and remembering that 2013 was scheduled as another election year, if the ETS was really considered electoral poison, they were pretty unlikely to have the guts to reintroduce it then.

Of course Rudd didn't need the ETS to force a double disso-lution; he had an alternative trigger in the twice-rejected health-insurance rebate means test. But it would be pretty hard to run a double-dissolution campaign without at least mentioning the ETS, and in the circumstances that could be an unwelcome distraction. All in all it was a spectacular political retreat and one which gave the Opposition its best line of attack to date. The challenge was all too simple: if Rudd believed in even half of what he had been saying for the last three years, then he should stick to his principles and call the election. If he wimped out, then he obviously didn't have any principles to stick to. It was Groucho Marx who made the immortal statement: 'These are my principles. If you don't like them, I have others.' The temptation to stick the appropriate spectacles, nose and moustache on our glorious leader was becoming irresistible.

Rudd's response that Tony Abbott had also changed his mind on supporting the ETS and that the Libs had welshed on the deal negotiated with Malcolm Turnbull was just not good enough. He, not Abbott, was supposed to be the saint, the man of the future, the one you could trust to do the right thing. Once again Rudd was being pulled back into the pack as just another opportunistic politician. He remained a better and more popular one than Abbott, but the gap was undoubtedly narrowing. The idea that the climate believers should persevere with him simply because he remained, marginally, the lesser of two evils was distinctly unappealing.

Rudd was elected in 2007 because he was seen to offer a positive alternative to the time-worn and directionless government of John Howard; it was time for a change and Rudd offered the prospect of moving forward, or at the very least catching up. No one wanted or expected a revolution, but there was a general belief that Rudd would be serious about the contemporary issues Howard had largely ignored: innovation and technology such as broadband, reform of the outdated federal system in health and education, and above all climate change. The global financial crisis disrupted the program somewhat, but it was also the making of Rudd; it reinforced his image as a decisive leader who could be trusted to act when the need arose. Even after the ascension of Abbott at the end of 2009, he appeared unassailable. Now, presumably at the behest of the pollsters, sociologists, minders, spin doctors, psephologists, astrologers and other crazies with whom he chose to surround himself, he had tossed it all away. It left him precious little to fall back on.

In the meantime Abbott had made another of his headland speeches, this time on foreign affairs. It had been largely swamped by the football fracas, which was perhaps just as well, because Abbott's view represented a monumental step backwards. Where Rudd was a true internationalist, seeking to engage with the rest of the world through as many multinational arrangements as were consonant with Australia's national interest, Abbott wanted to retreat beneath the shelter of the ANZUS umbrella; as long as the bilateral treaty with the United States was in place, the rest of the world could go jump. He did foreshadow an increase in Australia's commitment to the war in Afghanistan – as Washington had requested. But apart from that, it was back to fortress Australia. He even proposed acquiring a force of spy planes to guard against any threat to the oil and gas rigs off Western Australia, and, of course, the unimaginable peril of boats bearing asylum seekers.

Rudd's commitments would be unceremoniously scrapped. Australia would abandon its bid for a seat on the United Nations Security Council and downgrade its association with the international body. Rudd's International Commission on Nuclear Non-proliferation and Disarmament would be scrapped, as would his plans for an Asia-Pacific community. And aid would be largely restricted to the neighbourhood – the Pacific islands and some of the more deserving bits of Asia. It would be just like the Howard years, really – or perhaps even the Menzies years. Speaking of which, wasn't it time to get tougher with the dole bludgers? The dole could perhaps be refused, he mused to an audience of mining moguls, for those under thirty who were unwilling to leave their friends and move to the west for a job in the mines. One of the mining bosses gently broke it to him that it was no longer a matter of picking up a shovel and going out to load sixteen tons; the labour shortage was actually about skilled people, not just press-ganging youths off the streets. But Abbott remained keen on the idea: surely they could learn. He'd teach the bastards.

Rudd, on the other hand, was looking very long-term. In the wake of Anzac Day 2010, he announced plans for a commission to work out how to celebrate the centenary in 2015, by which time he would be well into his third term of office. His optimism extended to his appointment of commissioners: Bob Hawke, eighty-one, and Malcolm Fraser, seventy-nine. Age, it was hoped, shall not weary them. And to cap off the week, he announced that cigarette packets would lose their lustre and that their contents should become much more expensive. Cigs up! How traditional was that?

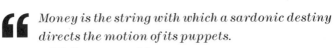

*Money is the string with which a sardonic destiny
directs the motion of its puppets.*
—W. SOMERSET MAUGHAM

WELL, QUITE TRADITIONAL enough, apparently. Beer, the
other half of the hallowed quinella, did not go up. When Ken
Henry's 'root and branch' report on the tax system at last hit the
deck, a volumetric tax on alcohol (which would have increased
the price of draught beer, as well as wine) was one of the many
recommendations Rudd ruled right out. Others included an
end to negative gearing, restoration of excise indexation for
petrol and diesel, a universal land tax, a means test on the
family home, and anything else that could have attracted more
than a whisper of opposition if Tony Abbott decided to use it as
part of a scare campaign about Rudd's secret re-election plans.
Abbott, of course, used them anyway, pointing out that Rudd
had broken his 2007 promise not to means test the private
health-insurance rebate and was therefore not to be trusted.

Most of Henry's other ideas were left in abeyance; his
138-item program was an immense one and would take at
least a decade to implement in full, even assuming that any
government had the guts to give it a try. Wayne Swan made
vague noises about a continuous process of reform as and

when circumstances permitted, and there were a few studied leaks about possible pre-election proposals, as long as they were not only worthy but immensely popular. Rudd did, however, adopt one of Henry's big ones, albeit in a modified form: as forecast, there would be what Abbott predictably deplored as a great big new tax on miners. What was described as their 'super profits,' that is, takings over and above the current bond rate, would be hit at the rate of 40 per cent. As always where Rudd was concerned, there would be concessions; up to 40 per cent of miners' initial expenses would be government guaranteed, to minimise the risk involved in new investment. And the $9 billion the government expected to make from the exercise would not be squirrelled away for a rainy day or put into a fund to be tapped when the mining boom came to an end, but would be spent on useful projects: an overall reduction of company tax, the build-up of infrastructure (especially the roads, railways and ports the miners were demanding) and additional superannuation for the workers.

It was a worthwhile package, and one hard to criticise. Given that the miners themselves had suggested a super profits tax in their 2008 submission to the Henry review, it should have come as no real surprise; the Minerals Council of Australia had suggested that a national profits-based tax on its members could be used to cut the rate of overall company tax, which was exactly what the government was now proposing.

But the miners, conveniently amnesiac in the manner of Alan Bond or Alexander Downer, went ballistic: investment would lurch to a halt, mines would close down, prospectors would pack their swags and the diggers would be forced to down tools and join the dole queues. The projects from which BHP Billiton and Rio Tinto were extracting (and exporting) squillions each year would simply disappear from the face of

Australia. The miners used words like socialism and national-isation; the excitable Clive Palmer described the policy as 'frankly communistic' and announced that he was cancelling a project which turned out not to have existed in the first place. The Western Australian Julie Bishop, the Liberals' Deputy Leader for Life, compared Rudd to Marx – Karl, not Groucho.

It was at this stage that Crikey came up with the headline: 'How can you tell when the miners are lying? They issue a press release.' Because, of course, the miners had form. They had predicted doom and disaster back in 1985 at the introduc-tion of a similar tax on the petroleum industry, which was now flourishing as never before. They had said they would pick up their bongos and go home at the first mention of an emissions trading scheme; indeed, any worthwhile action on climate change would mean a total shut-down of the industry. No one, except perhaps Tony Abbott, took them seriously. Abbott agreed that Rudd's proposal would kill the mining industry and sat down with the head honcho of BHP Billiton, Marius Kloppers, and his Rio Tinto counterpart, David Peever, in Canberra to work on their forthcoming scare campaign. Cynical observers suggested that the miners arrived with carpet bags.

Rudd, in the meantime, set out for the west to talk to another collection of movers and shakers and was presented by his erst-while ally 'Twiggy' Forrest of Fortescue Metals with a pair of boxing gloves inscribed with *Fair suck of the sauce bottle, mate* – a pointed correction to Rudd's earlier mangling of the Austral-ian idiom, but also an indication that the gloves were now off. Rudd was reportedly surprised at the vehemence of the miners. He asked for facts and figures, which were not forthcoming; but threats certainly were. So, with determined timidity he promised to listen to their concerns (doing so earlier might have been more productive) and to consider each individual case on its merits. To anyone acquainted with Rudd's methods of negotiation, this meant granting concessions at the taxpayers' expense, and only added to the impression that the prime minister was primarily concerned with buying off opposition rather than making hard decisions and sticking to them. This was a bit tough, because by and large Rudd's initial response to the Henry report was both good policy and good politics. But because it came when the government was perceived to be in full retreat on a number of fronts, it got little credit. The commentators were more concerned with the reforms Rudd had squibbed than the ones to which he was committed, and accused him of continuing to run scared. The taint of political cowardice, once acquired, is a hard one to shake.

And it bites with the voters like a maddened piranha. Newspoll was taken before the Henry report and Rudd's response, so if there was to be any bounce for the government it would not have shown up. But it certainly took in the reaction to the shelving of the ETS, and it appeared that climate change was still a trigger issue with a lot of people. Wayne Swan bravely suggested that the 8 per cent drop in Labor's primary vote should be blamed on smokers protesting against the price rise, which suggested he was smoking something else altogether. Labor's primary support was down to 35 per cent, with the Coalition's up three to 43 per cent; this put Labor in a losing position on the two-party-preferred vote for the first time since Kevin Rudd became leader. Rudd's own popularity had fallen by a mammoth eleven points, from a net rating of plus nine to minus eleven. And suddenly more voters saw Tony Abbott as decisive and strong than they did Rudd, and the government's lead as the best party to handle climate change had evaporated.

Desperate to salvage something from the wreck, Labor strategists pointed out that Rudd's fall had not resulted in a substantial rise for Abbott; most of the lost Labor vote had gone not to the Coalition or even the Greens, but to the mysterious 'others.' Satisfaction with Abbott's performance had actually fallen slightly, from plus six to plus two, and Rudd was still comfortably ahead as preferred prime minister. The punters may have gone cool on the idea of Rudd, but that did not mean they wanted Abbott as their leader. The fairest interpretation of the poll seemed to be that it was a 'plague on both your houses' affair. And, of course, it could have had a rogue element. Serious observers felt it would be wise to suspend judgment for at least a fortnight; perhaps the budget would straighten things out.

There were quite a few backbenchers who were very anxious that it should. A number of those in marginal seats had been tipped the wink to be ready to move quickly: parliament would not be resuming after it rose on 24 June and it might not last that long. The session due to begin on 23 August was definitely off. This was surprising, because it suggested that Rudd was gearing up for a double dissolution after all; if he wasn't, there was no point in going so early. Yet by trying to kill off the ETS as an issue, he appeared to have rejected the double dissolution option. But then, our beloved prime minister had always been a bit difficult to interpret.

And so was the share market. Mining stocks dropped dramatically after Rudd's initial announcement but lurched back up next day, and the big brokers – Macquarie, Goldman-Sachs and JBWere among them – all considered that they remained a good buy. BHP Billiton and Rio Tinto both spread stories about cutting down on their Australian operations, but it was not clear whether this was more bluff or, if it wasn't, whether it was really due to Rudd's announcement – companies of that size seldom take big decisions with quite such alacrity. A couple of smaller players were more explicit: Tony Sage, executive chairman of Cape Lambert Resources, announced that he would pull out of his embryonic operation in Western Australia and move to the more rapeable territory of West Africa. Given that analysts were forecasting that his company would be out of cash altogether within six weeks, it seemed improbable that a prospective tax on super profits had much to do with the decision. It later turned out that Sage, having talked his company's share price down, then bought shares himself at the bargain-basement price, a practice which would have entailed his incarceration under any even mildly ethical system. The miners then went public, taking out full-page newspaper advertisements insisting that they actually gave a lot back to Australia because, hey, they paid tax, just like everyone else – the implication was that they really shouldn't have to, but they did it anyway. And it was true: they paid quite a lot of tax because their profits were enormous. This was due less to their own efforts than to the fact that commodity prices had skyrocketed in recent times. The increased demand, especially from China, had led to enormous windfall profits. For them to start crying poor now was, well, a bit rich. Kloppers appealed to sweet reason; the industry, he said, did not really object to a resources rent tax as such, but it should only apply to future projects, not to the ones that were already yielding the super profits. But hang on – it was precisely these future projects that Kloppers and his mates were saying were in danger of cancellation because of the new tax. Their logic was, to put it mildly, a trifle hard to follow.

At this stage the debate was largely sound and fury, but there was one disturbing undercurrent. In pushing his case for the new tax, Rudd made much of the fact that a lot of the miners' profits went offshore. BHP Billiton was 40 per cent foreign owned and Rio Tinto 70 per cent. But our minerals were 100 per cent Australian and proud of it, and true blue Aussies should be the ones benefiting from their exploitation. It wasn't quite as crude as that: his actual wording was, 'these massively increased profits built on Australian resources are mostly, in fact, going overseas.' But the message was clear enough: economic jingoism, for which Opposition figures such as Barnaby Joyce had rightly been derided, was suddenly on the government's agenda. And it was not a welcome one. Charles Blunt, chief executive of the American Chamber of Commerce in Australia, immediately warned that Rudd's comments raised the issue of whether Australia remained a predictable and welcoming destination for foreign investment. Given that Australia has always relied on foreign investment to promote its development and growth and will continue to do so for the foreseeable future, this was serious stuff.

For Rudd of all people to indulge in dog-whistling xenophobia was truly frightening. This was supposed to be the gutter politics indulged in by the Liberals, with Tony Abbott's vendettas against asylum seekers and indeed against immigrants in general; Abbott had now declared that reducing immigration would be a key part of his election platform, and we all knew what this could mean for unscrupulous candidates in certain electorates. In case there was any doubt, the Coalition unveiled the first of its television advertisements, which showed that Abbott had not forgotten the lessons learned from his mentor, Bartholomew Augustine Santamaria. The ads were straight out the Democratic Labor Party's manual from the 1960s: Australia was being invaded by huge and sinister red arrows originating from somewhere in Asia. This time the arrows were mad Moslem asylum seekers rather than communist infiltrators, but the message was the same: Australia's way of life – no, our very survival as a nation – was under threat, and Rudd was doing nothing about it. Abbott would take Real Action. Just what action was unclear, but his parliamentary secretary Cory Bernardi gave us a clue when he launched yet another campaign to ban the burqa, which, he revealed, was the preferred disguise of bandits and ne'er-do-wells. Burqas had, it appeared, replaced balaclavas. The retiring (but not soon enough or far enough) Nick Minchin told a select audience that there was nothing wrong with WorkChoices – it was just that the electors didn't like it. The reports rather scotched rumours that John Singleton would be switching loyalties to the Abbott camp for the forthcoming campaign. Obviously Singo was a bit too subtle and sophisticated for the onslaught that was being planned. He would work for the miners instead.

In the circumstances it was rather refreshing to hear that Malcolm Turnbull had reversed his decision to leave politics, and that we were going to have him to kick around for a while yet. It was not clear just why the Lord of Vaucluse felt the public sector still had something to offer him. Abbott, putting a brave face on, claimed it was because Turnbull saw the Coalition had a chance of winning the election; others maintained that Turnbull figured the Coalition was doomed, and that when Abbott stepped down he would be given another chance. Rudd's dumping of the ETS was possibly a factor, as was the departure of Nick Minchin. But the most likely explanation is probably the simplest: Turnbull had responded to the pleas of friends and colleagues who wanted him not just for his undoubted talents, but because he was the party's best – perhaps only – chance of hanging on to the seat of Wentworth, now made marginal by the incursion of large numbers of gays and greenies.

Politics, once contracted, is a hard bug to shake, and Turnbull had unfinished business. At the very least his active presence would make things more interesting. He celebrated his recommitment with a newspaper article lambasting Rudd's indecision and political cowardice, which was fine as far as it went; but some of his colleagues would have been happier if he had also said something nice about his own leader and his policies. Perhaps, they suggested, more in hope than expectation, that would come later.

In any case, it seemed that his well-chosen words were superfluous: Rudd was doing a fine line in self-immolation without needing any outside help. The Nielsen poll released the day before the budget was even worse than the Newspoll of the previous week: Rudd's fall was steeper and faster than even the most pessimistic of his colleagues had expected. He now had a net approval rating of minus four, his first ever drop below the line, and Labor was looking at the loss of nineteen seats and government. Once again the silver lining, if you could call it that, was that Abbott was not doing much better and Rudd was still clearly ahead as preferred prime minister. But possibly the worst news of all was that the mining tax was actually a vote-loser. The effect was most obvious in Western Australia, where Labor support had dropped a massive ten points and was now an awful 25 per cent. But across the board, a small majority thought it was a bad idea. So much for the tactical geniuses from the New South Wales right who had sold it to Rudd as an infallible populist move. As so often, they had shown that they might be crash-hot at knee-capping, but from the shoulders up they were incapable of anything more subtle than a Liverpool kiss.

Perhaps in retaliation, Rudd announced that they, and all the other members of parliament, were to lose all their frequent-flyer points. That would teach them. And Labor members were also grounded for the rest of the session. They were to get out into their electorates and sell the government's amazing record of achievement, starting with the weathering of the global financial crisis, and coming to a climax with ... well, we would have to wait and see. In fact many backbenchers, especially those in marginal seats, were already thinking about their own survival, and ominously, the figure of Kevin Rudd was not prominent in their cogitations. Their glorious leader was no longer the unalloyed asset he had been in 2007; in many of their private polls, as in the public ones, he was starting to look like a distinct liability. Local campaign managers were already considering the old trick of presenting their charges as sort of Labor independents, which was not good news for Rudd in that it could only reinforce the negative cycle.

Inevitably, conversations in pubs were turning to Julia Gillard, and what an amazingly presentable and marketable candidate she would make. One brave reporter even asked Rudd, a first-term prime minister, the question that had bedevilled John Howard in his political dotage: if he were re-elected, would he guarantee to serve out the full term? Well, golly gosh and stuff me up a dead bear's bum. Did anyone seriously imagine otherwise? Rudd's program had always been a long-term one: many of his pet projects would not come to fruition for nearly a decade. In spite of the silly rumours that he saw the Lodge as a mere staging post on his way to the top job with the United Nations, he would be quite as hard to extract from his current position as any of his predecessors. When he did go, it would be kicking and screaming.

The upsurge of support for Gillard had been driven at least partly by Rudd's plunge in the opinion polls, which was in turn a result of his serial retreat from previously held policy positions. No one – well, no one who can count – was seriously suggesting that he would face a challenge before the election, but there was a school of thought developing that he would be eased out shortly thereafter.

It relied on the perception that Rudd was now irrevocably damaged; he could never regain the public's confidence, and it would be smart to make the transition before the voters really turned against him. And given Gillard's unquestioned popularity – her fan base now encompassed right and left, old and young, rich and poor, gay and straight – it would be sensible to exploit her sooner rather than later.

Her supporters pointed to the fact that, unlike Rudd, Gillard was admired even by the conservative commentariat: Alan Jones was an aficionado, and her weekly TV chats with Tony Abbott resembled those of a long-married couple who might have their disagreements, but would never say anything really nasty to each other.

However, the most remarkable confirmation of Gillard's political saleability was her treatment by that bastion of the right, the *Australian*. The national daily had conducted a series of campaigns against the Rudd government, but none had been so unremitting as those against its economic stimulus programs, in particular the home-insulation scheme and Building the Education Revolution. But there had been a key difference. In the first case, right from the start the paper had demanded the sacking of the responsible minister, Peter Garrett. But in the second case, there had been no suggestion that Gillard should fall on her sword.

The paper's attack on the BER had been obsessive, at times bordering on the psychotic; even after the audit that said the BER had largely succeeded in its basic aims of providing employment and improving education infrastructure, the *Australian*'s hit squad continued its frenzied assaults on every aspect of the scheme, insisting that it was widely loathed and despised by parents and schools alike.

In fact the audit declared that 95 per cent of school principals were happy with the results – nineteen in every twenty. You'd be lucky to get that sort of consensus about the pope being a Catholic. The malcontents the *Australian* was trotting out as typical of their group were revealed as an insignificant minority. This did not stop its commentators from insisting that the whole idea had been an unqualified disaster.

The idea, yes; but not its instigator and administering minister, who was still seen as one of the saving graces of a government to whose destruction the Murdoch press was dedicated.

One saving grace, but not the only one. Unlike the Coalition, Labor had a front bench of considerable competence and ambition. Gillard was obviously the front-runner, but Wayne Swan, Stephen Smith and Lindsay Tanner wouldn't mind a crack at the prize, and further back in the field Craig Emerson, Tony Burke, Greg Combet (fulsomely featured in the *Australian*'s weekend magazine) and Bill Shorten had their aspirations too. In the case of the latter group, the longer a change of leadership was delayed the better. Rudd would have to fall much further before there was any real risk of rebellion. But it didn't stop the rumours: even Bob Hawke was forced to issue a statement denying a report (based on a piece of eavesdropping by a Liberal staffer) that he had discussed the possibility of a pre-election switch. And the pollsters got in on the act, including Gillard in their questions about whom the public wanted as prime minister. Rudd remained the first choice for most, although one online poll suggested Gillard would have won if the voting system were preferential and if Lindsay Tanner and Wayne Swan had also been candidates. But Gillard strenuously and convincingly denied that she was making a run. That, of course, mattered not one wit to the tabloids, who were frothing at the mouth at the prospect of a leadership contest between a feisty, sexy, photogenic red-haired sheila and a grey, smart-arse nerd. For Labor's real powerbrokers it was another unwelcome distraction. But among the rank and file there was a lot of nervousness developing. So far Rudd's fall from grace had only sporadically been reflected in overall voting intentions; things looked a bit grim, but not irreparably so. However, Rudd was undeniably the public face of the government, and would inevitably become even more so as the campaign developed. Would the disillusionment with the prime minister spread to envelop the whole of brand Labor?

The worries about Rudd's public standing had crystallised around the deferral of the ETS, and every week brought more evidence that this was not only a panicky political overreaction but also a seriously bad idea. As the sceptics, led by the industry-subsidised propagandists of the Institute of Public Affairs and their funereal mouthpiece John Roskam, were triumphantly claiming victory for ignorance and apathy, 255 of America's most reputable scientists published a plea for a return to rational discussion: the problem, they claimed, was too urgent and important to be hijacked by extremists and demagogues. Australia's chief scientist, Penny Sackett, issued her own call for the government to show leadership and commitment. And the most telling criticism of Rudd's procrastination came from China, where Professor Pan Jiahua, described as a leading adviser to the Politburo, said Rudd's decision had the effect of discouraging developing nations from implementing measures to contain emissions. Australia was already doing much less than China about the problem, and the message it was sending to the developing world was: 'If even an industrialised country like Australia can't do it, how can we?' Quite.

Amid all this, for some of us at least there was one positive note. The formation of the National Congress of Australia's First Peoples, the representative body to replace the Aboriginal and Torres Strait Islander Commission as a national indigenous forum, was a sign that the great issue of reconciliation was still on the government's agenda. Unlike ATSIC the new body would be at arm's length from government and its structure ensured that it could not be taken over by a political clique; it recognised that individual delegates could only represent their own tribal groups (or nations) and could not presume to speak for the Aboriginal people as a whole, any more than the president of, say Portugal, could claim to represent the whole of Europe. In both a concrete and a symbolic sense, NCAFP would fill the vacuum the abolition of ATSIC had left, and return a voice to the indigenous population.

That was the good news. Unfortunately it was not the kind of news to knock the government's polling woes out of the headlines. Pre-budget media stories are usually full of contrived leaks, setting the scene for a grand unveiling and a jubilant treasurer. But in 2010 Wayne Swan deliberately dampened expectations: this was to be a responsible, conservative budget, not an election-year bonanza. The risk was that with Labor seen to be accident-prone at best and out of control at worst, and with a prime minister in free fall, whatever was in Tuesday's document would be reported as a last desperate gambit from a government on the skids. As it turned out it wasn't reported thus, not even by the *Australian*. It hardly set the nation on fire, either. But then, it was never intended to. The first reaction to the budget was ho, and the second was hum – which was exactly the way Kevin Rudd and Wayne Swan wanted it. The headline they were hoping for might have read: 'Very quiet budget, not many hurt.' If the populace had poured into the streets laughing, cheering and weeping with delight, they would have known that something was wrong, that they had been populist and irresponsible. Their ambition was for the budget to be seen as firm but fair, and by and large they succeeded.

The declaration that the surplus would be restored three years earlier than predicted was undoubtedly good news, but it was never going to be the occasion for spontaneous expressions of joy and gratitude by the voters; and nor should it have been, because it was much more the result of accident than careful economic planning. The accident was last year's forward estimates, which were so wildly wrong as to suggest that it might be an idea if Julia Gillard extended her NAPLAN numeracy testing to include the boffins of Treasury. The 2009 figures were derided at the time as making heroic assumptions about the speed of Australia's recovery from the global financial crisis; they were now revealed as pessimistic and petty to the point of absurdity. Certainly the rivers of gold from China helped, but it also turned out that the government's stimulus measures were far more successful in arresting unemployment than had been predicted, and the government was also able to defy the cynics by curbing, if not actually cutting, its spending.

In other words a lot of things that Treasury thought likely to go wrong actually went right. For once, Murphy's Law broke down. Which of course raised the question: if the estimates were so hopelessly awry last year, why should we believe them this year? Well, partly because things appeared to be a bit more predictable; in spite of the turmoil in Greece and the risk of it spreading around Europe, the recovery was now unambiguously under way and Australia was at the head of the pack, with government debt and deficit figures minuscule by international standards. And the prognosis for revenue seemed soundly based; while there was always a chance something disastrous would happen to the Chinese economy, demand from India was steadily increasing and global reliance on coal and iron ore was not going to fall away anytime soon.

The real shock of the pre-budget Nielsen poll had been the finding that more voters opposed the new resources tax than supported it, a statistic so contrary to the normal Australian tradition of cutting down the tall poppies that it seemed hard to credit. Obviously, Rudd was hoping for a boost from the tax and the budget, but it appeared that Abbott, with his knee-jerk opposition to the great big new tax which would kill the goose that laid the golden eggs, would be the one to get it. Certainly he emerged from his talks with BHP Billiton's Kloppers and Rio Tinto's Peever with the satisfied expression of a party leader who had put all his funding worries behind him for the foreseeable future. And in his budget reply speech he delivered in spades – that being the miner's preferred suit. It is a peculiar Australian convention that although the real treasurer delivers the budget, the shadow treasurer does not reply to it: the starring role is usurped by the Opposition leader. In 2010 this was a pity, because not only would Joe Hockey have been funnier, but we would have been spared the spectacle of Tony Abbott trying to be statesmanlike; disappointingly, he did not appear in his budget smugglers. His diatribes against what fanciers of exotic wildlife interpret as the Grey Pig Newt Axe were, of course, predictable, and the only new lines were promises to freeze the public service (actually the Canberra winters are already quite cold enough) and to reduce government advertising; given that the present government had already cut this to half what it was under John Howard, the pledge was somewhat underwhelming.

Government ministers, especially Lindsay Tanner, who had apparently appointed himself as Abbott's nemesis, criticised the effort as a meaningless collection of negativity, slogans and sound-bites. Certainly it was a bit thin on content, but Abbott came across, if not quite as a statesman, then at least as a coherent and articulate campaigner. The relief on his own side was obvious.

Many years ago a radio pundit named Eric Baume was famous for delivering passionate denunciations of just about everything. After one such effort, Baume asked his producer what he thought of the speech.

'Well,' replied the producer, 'it was bullshit.'

Baume gleamed through his spectacles. 'Ah, yes,' he chortled. 'But it was good bullshit.'

Tony Abbott was emerging as a demagogue in the same mould.

> *I've never had anyone put on a puppet show to convince me of anything.* — GARRY SHANDLING

 9.

NATIONAL POLITICS had taken an unexpected turn. Increasingly, both Rudd *and* Abbott were seen by the public as objects of ridicule. Neither leader did much to retrieve the situation in their immediate post-budget appearances. Rudd, in response to some unusually hostile questioning from the *7.30 Report*'s Kerry O'Brien, lost his cool and addressed his interrogator sarcastically as 'mate' in the same threatening tones used by the New South Wales right; Bill Hayden once remarked that being called 'mate' by the right was like coming home to find a severed horse's head on your bed. The incident was natural enough and in other circumstances might have been to Rudd's credit: he was a normal human being, after all. But in the circumstances it was taken as a symptom of instability, a sign that Rudd was out of control. Abbott had his own moment of humiliation with the normally supportive Neil Mitchell on Melbounre radio 3AW: quizzed about a story that he had wanted to include an annual payment of $10,000 for stay-at-home mothers in his budget reply speech but had been rolled by his colleagues, he blustered, blathered and dithered and eventually admitted he was a wimp.

In fact the story was true, and the idea remained on his agenda as a possible future announcement. But it was easy to see why it had been postponed: Abbott was already having trouble with his sums. With Rudd and Swan campaigning on a platform of economic responsibility and austerity, it was difficult for Abbott to follow his normal political instinct, which was to splash out the goodies and let someone else worry about the cost. That someone else was to be Joe Hockey, who had been loaded with the responsibility of explaining just where the money was coming from in the weeks ahead. Abbott had already ruled out Rudd's promises of company-tax relief, new infrastructure and the superannuation increase, which were funded partly or wholly by the resources super profit tax (RSPT). He had also promised to can the National Broadband Network, but the government insisted that this was not a saving, because the NBN was actually an investment which would eventually pay for itself. And Lindsay Tanner claimed to have documented proof that Abbott was already up the spout for some $15.7 billion worth of unfunded promises before the campaign had even started. Quite suddenly the electoral battleground had shifted again. Only a fortnight earlier it had been all about health and hospitals, which was where Rudd wanted it; then it had switched to the mining tax, which was where Abbott wanted it. Now the field had spread out further, into the simple-sounding but all-encompassing argument: it's the economy, stupid.

And the lines of attack were becoming depressingly clear: it was going to be a very negative campaign. The conservatives would portray Rudd as unprincipled and untrustworthy, a coward and an opportunist who wanted to tax the productive side of the economy out of existence to fund wasteful and worthless schemes. Labor had already branded Abbott as flaky, erratic, innumerate, fanatical and downright dangerous, the kind of crazy you wouldn't trust with your dog, let alone your country. Any hope of vision or idealism looked set to disappear in an unedifying shitfight, the theme of which would be: 'Our man might be pretty suss, but look at the other fruitcake.' Or, as one Labor minister summed it up: 'They're pissed off with us, but they think he's a crazy bastard.' Ah, the joys of serious political debate in Australia. It was horrible, but in a sense understandable; with the economic imperative being a race to get the budget back in surplus as soon as possible, neither side could buy its way out of trouble, and there were signs that the voters were getting sick of what they saw as airy-fairy promises anyway. If they couldn't have something concrete, they might just settle for stability.

Thus the game was all about proving that the other lot would upset things more than you would. The Labor hardheads believed that when the crunch came, the swinging voters would decide that while Abbott might be lots of fun to have around, they didn't really want him in charge, and that would be that. But the private polling of both parties showed that things were getting pretty tight in the marginal seats, especially in New South Wales and Queensland, which was where Labor could lose government. Backbenchers were praying that Rudd would finally pull his finger out, and that when he did the punters would still be listening. At least he had their undivided attention when he welcomed the teenage round-the-world sailor Jessica Watson home, declaring her 'Australia's latest hero.' In tune with the times, she immediately disagreed: 'I'm no hero.' Oh dear, couldn't he even get that right? And even the redoubtable Abby appeared out of sorts during the RSPCA's Million Paws Walk. Given that the Rudd household had bragged of her almost supernatural intuition, this was a dire omen indeed.

On the other hand, things weren't looking too bright on the Coalition side either. Shadow Health Minister Peter Dutton had been sprung buying mining shares at the same time as his leader was declaring that the government's tax proposal had made them entirely worthless – hardly an expression of solidarity. And the Liberals' serial shonk Michael Johnson was finally facing expulsion over a succession of suspect financial deals. This was excellent news for Labor, as Johnson announced his intention to carry on as an 'Independent Liberal,' giving Labor a good chance of winning his marginal seat of Ryan. Abbott, who had previously offered Johnson his personal support, still refused to condemn him. And the ex-Nats and ex-Libs now forcibly united in the Queensland Liberal–National Party stepped up their internecine brawling. Suddenly the Sunshine State was looking much sunnier for Labor. The shadow treasurer, Joe Hockey, appeared in a one-to-one *Q&A* with Finance Minister Lindsay Tanner (Wayne Swan was busy arguing with the miners in Perth) and chortled his way through a somewhat boring hour of television; he seemed incapable of taking questions about the economy seriously. But then Tony Abbott appeared on the *7.30 Report* for what was expected to be a routine interview with Kerry O'Brien, and the chortling abruptly stopped.

Richard Nixon declared certain of his statements inoperative. George Bush sometimes misspoke. John Howard had his core and non-core promises. And Winston Churchill admitted occasionally being guilty of a terminological inexactitude. Now Tony Abbott took his rightful place in this pantheon of weasel-worded mendacity by confessing that some of his policy pronouncements were not entirely consistent. What he said in the heat of the moment should not always be taken with the same degree of assurance as what he read from carefully scripted documents. Or something like that. As his attempts to explain his position to an incredulous Kerry O'Brien continued, he became Jesuitical to the point of incomprehensibility. It was not, as he agreed later in a moment of indisputable candour, his finest interview.

And the real stupidity of it was that all he had to do was say that he had changed his mind; that the weight of evidence had persuaded him that the need for a comprehensive, firmly funded system of parental care was sufficiently urgent for him to abandon his earlier ritual pledge of no new taxes. Red Kezza would still have given him a working over, but at least he would not have been lumbered with Phoney Tony for the rest of his career, and he would not have been subject to the harassment he was going to get from government and media alike every time he said anything purportedly serious from that moment on. And of course, he would not have had the embarrassment of Barnaby Joyce trying to help him out: 'What someone might say to their lover in the heat of passion should be entirely different to what you would say to the lady checking out your groceries at the supermarket.' Oh, I don't know: 'Do you take American Express?' would seem to cover both situations.

Assessing Abbott's credibility on any given occasion was going to be even more difficult than he had suggested. Reading from his carefully scripted budget reply speech the previous week, he had stated – even promised – that the Opposition's proposed spending cuts would be fully detailed by Joe Hockey at the Press Club. Nothing heat-of-the-moment about it: this was a serious and considered commitment. Or so the prima donnas of the press gallery believed when they fronted on Wednesday, only to find that Hockey had flick-passed the commitment to Andrew Robb. Instead Hockey blandly announced a grand total of $46.7 billion in cuts and went on to give a talk on what he somewhat grandiosely described as his economic philosophy. The hacks took this as a serious affront, and unanimously decided that Hockey's failure to deliver was the real story; what he actually had to say was no longer relevant. Robb did belatedly appear to hand out a list of proposed savings, and to answer a few questions, but the news coverage centred on Abbott and Hockey's unforgivable snubbing of the people who really run things in Canberra.

The anger set the tone for what serious coverage there was: Robb's list was derided as ill-informed and misleading, in that it consisted largely of axing proposals that were not even on the drawing board, like the proposed cuts in company tax and the sell-off of capital assets such as Medicare Private. Even many of the current programs that were to be axed, like Building the Education Revolution, would be replaced by others in the same field which could, as Robb proudly admitted, be even more expensive. Independent economists estimated the total real savings as somewhere between 5 and 8 billion dollars, which did not even cover the cost of Coalition promises already announced; items like Abbott's direct action on climate change wouldn't come cheap.

The *Australian*, as always, tried to do its bit. Under Hockey's headline figure of $46.7 billion it published a list of everything that could conceivably be regarded as a saving and quite a few things that couldn't. Even so, the total only came to $42.6 billion – but hey, what's a few billion between close friends? It seemed likely that Merry Andrew would soon join Phoney Tony and Sloppy Joe in the Labor lexicon of economic shadow ministers who could not be taken seriously. It might, as some brave souls were suggesting, even be time to bring Malcolm Turnbull back into the fold; at least he knew something about money.

This was obviously one area of vulnerability for the Coalition; another was that it was rapidly painting itself into a corner over what Abbott continued, gratingly, to call Rudd's great big new tax. The miners' public opposition was vigorous and unremitting, but behind the scenes a lot of negotiating was going on and the government was getting some high-powered support from Ken Henry in Treasury, whose defence of the tax was comprehensive and passionate, and from Ross Garnaut, arguably the country's most respected economic planner, who described it as elegant, if badly sold and in need of the odd tweak. GetUp!'s supportive advertising campaign wasn't hurting either.

Most of the hardheads accepted that some sort of resources rent tax was inevitable; the only question was how much ground the government was prepared to give. Almost certainly the answer was, not much; the political imperative was not to be seen to be backing down in the face of threats and bluster based on pure self-interest. Clearly the government wanted to resolve the issue as quickly as possible, and given that the ongoing uncertainty was not doing the miners much good either, it was more likely than not that an agreement would emerge before the election, especially if the government regained its lead in the polls. A Rudd victory would be seen as a popular mandate for the new tax and, in any case, the Coalition was all but certain to lose its power to block legislation in the Senate; a Labor–Green majority would see the changes passed without delay. If agreement could be reached, even one that made concessions to the miners, it would inevitably be seen as a win for the government; which would leave Abbott, yet again, without a central issue.

To be consistent, he would have to continue to oppose what would still be a great big new tax on the mining industry, even if it ended up being in a form that the industry accepted. But as the week had conclusively demonstrated, Abbott was not obsessively concerned with consistency. He could, however, do a good line in passion. The RSPT was 'almost criminal'; it had by now morphed into a battle between good and evil, something approaching a religious crusade: you almost expected to hear him declare it the greatest moral, social and economic challenge of our times. Fortunately the rest of his party did not see it like that. Some at least were aware that sooner or later the hysteria would have to die down and the real debate begin. At that point passion would not be enough.

By the end of the week the hard questions were finally being asked about just how much tax the miners actually paid now and how much they were going to pay if the new regime came into being. The quick answer was, obviously, as little as they could get away with, and it appeared that this would be considerably less than their advertising claimed.

For a start, it ignored the fact that state royalties would effectively be abolished under Rudd's changes. It did not take into account that the government would pick up 40 per cent of their exploration and establishment costs, nor that many miners – the ones who did not make super profits – would not pay the tax at all. And it also glossed over the very generous concessions they received under the present system, and would continue to receive if and when the new one came into operation. The miners' headline figure was that they now paid an effective rate of 43 per cent and that this would increase to 57 per cent. Now this was disputed: an American study quoted in the Henry report put the figure at 13 per cent for the multinationals and 17 per cent for the natives, small enough to convince other enterprises and individuals, who paid around the standard rate of 30 per cent, that the miners were not, as the government continually averred, paying their fair share.

On behalf of the mining industry, Andrew Robb dismissed the study as the shonkiest thing he'd ever seen because it lumped New Zealand in with Australia and was the work of a student – well, a graduate student actually, one Kevin Markle, who had collaborated on it with Professor Doug Shackelford, a world authority on the subject, who had spent several years conducting the most comprehensive comparative study of international tax rates ever made. However, as a rather bemused Shackelford pointed out when contacted in Tanzania, it did not provide a definitive analysis of individual cases. Gotcha, said the miners, because it didn't cover royalties and it was wrong anyway. They triumphantly waved figures obtained from the Tax Office, which put the rate at 27.8 per cent, which, they crowed, was higher than the industry average.

True, but this was because the average was pulled down by the huge size of the lightly taxed financial sector. In fact the mining sector was sixteenth on the list of twenty-one provided by the office, paying less than comparable industries such as manufacturing and construction. Well, yes, responded the miners, but we also pay royalties, which brings the effective rate up to 41.3 per cent – not, it should be noted, the 43 per cent they had claimed in their advertisements: this turned out to be a reference to their taxable income, not the tax they actually paid, but what the hell. Craig Sainsbury of Citigroup said that in fact it was under 35 per cent, and as has been pointed out, whatever figure was used, it ignored the fact that the royalties were to be absorbed in the proposed new system, and also that the miners, unlike other industries, received huge tax concessions, such as fuel subsidies and depreciation allowances. Taking these into account, said Wayne Swan, triumphantly waving his own paper obtained from the Treasury, the actual tax paid over the last eight years indeed came down to 17 per cent. So there.

George Megalogenis drew all this together in a telling piece in the *Australian*, which the paper published as a side bar to its main story, 'Swan tax claims undermined,' a diatribe which failed to mention most of the analysis made by its sole remaining credible journalist. The paper preferred the view of John Ralph, a retired mining executive who stated baldly that the new tax would be against the national interest, so there. Increasingly our national daily resembled a huge advertorial, with full-page paid advertisements from the miners interlarded with self-interested waffle posing as news content.

By this stage literally scores of respectable economists were on the record as saying the RSPT, perhaps with a little tweaking, was undeniably a good thing. On any rational level, the government should have been winning the argument; the only real opposition was coming from the miners themselves, clearly driven by self-interest, and from the Coalition, who just thought it was good politics. The campaign should never have gained political traction. Not only did the miners have form – they had cried wolf when their super profits were threatened in the past – but the claims they made were badly misleading, if not downright lies. As Treasury Secretary Ken Henry pointed out to a Senate estimates committee, they did not save Australia from recession; in fact, unlike the economy as a whole, they fell into it themselves. They sacked more than 15 per cent of their workers; if all other employers had been as ruthless, unemployment would have jumped from under 5 per cent to over 19 per cent.

The tax was not retrospective: past profits were not affected, only future ones. Tax rates change all the time, and established businesses and individuals cannot claim that they are retrospective simply because the rate was something else when they were established or born. The alcopops tax was not considered retrospective, although alcopops were already being manufactured and marketed when it was introduced. Even on a local level, council rates can change and houses built when they were at a low level can suddenly find themselves subject to increased charges. To call the changes retrospective was to distort the language.

And most importantly, the new tax would not see the miners paying 57 per cent tax – the highest taxing regime of any country, as they moaned – unless their profit levels reached an extraordinary 50 per cent, at which point it might be said that they could afford to give a bit of it back. If they made a healthy 10 per cent, they would in fact be paying less than they are now. The hard fact was that because commodity prices had risen fantastically in the past few years, the miners were now paying only about half what they used to, and this was not fair. End of story. So why was the government so defensive?

Well, because, as the ETS campaign – or lack of one – showed, its ministers couldn't sell a cold beer in the Simpson Desert. Rudd and his troops seemed incapable of putting their case in terms the public could relate to. In parliament, Rudd rabbited on about cuts to company tax and increases to superannuation that would flow from the new revenue. Few, if any, gave a stuff. They were more worried about the alleged threats to their existing super funds and the collapse of the share market. The falls on stock exchanges around the world had nothing at all to do with the proposed RSPT; they were, of course, due to the chaos in Europe. In fact mining stocks had weathered the storm better than most. But none of this was getting through to the punters. On the contrary, the polls showed that the more Rudd and his ministers ranted, the more their arguments were ignored.

The only people really paying attention were the backbenchers in the mining seats. Barry Haase, the Liberal member for

O'Connor, centred on the mining town of Kalgoorlie, was jubilant, actually describing the Treasury figures on tax as 'rubbery.' Even Steve Irons, whose seat of Swan had been made notionally Labor after a redistribution, could afford to smile. But Labor's Sharryn Jackson in Hasluck risked being caught in the backlash, which was predictably strongest in Western Australia. Polling showed that even Gary Gray in Brand, with a margin of more than 6 per cent, was at risk. And in Queensland, Leichhardt, Dawson and Flynn were all marginal Labor with a large mining component. If Rudd could not turn things around before the election, his failure to sell the RSPT alone could cost at least five seats, pushing his government right to the edge. As a preliminary measure, he cancelled an appointment to attend the annual dinner of the Minerals Council of Australia.

So, faced with the very real prospect of snatching defeat from the jaws of victory, the master strategists of the Labor Party finally called in the professionals, a move which was politically desperate and morally dubious and which, with the government already on the nose, could well provoke a public backlash. In Opposition, Rudd had rightly inveighed against the misuse of taxpayer funds for political advertising by John Howard and promised to end the practice. Since then he had commissioned ads about his health reforms which many felt stretched the limits, but at least they conformed to the guidelines his government had set. It was most unlikely the new lot would pass the same test; indeed, the government exempted them from even having to try. Abbott, as a relic of the Howard years, was hardly in a position to complain (although he did anyway) but the long-suffering taxpayers had every right to feel they had been conned yet again. The government's excuse was that the public was hungry for information and something had to be done to counteract the misleading propaganda from the miners. Well, perhaps, but it was a pity that Rudd and his ministers had proved to be too incompetent to do it themselves. Instead they called in the agencies and told them to make up the lost ground.

And there was a lot of ground to make up. In one week alone we had been told authoritatively that the miners' effective tax rate was 13 per cent, 14 per cent, 17 per cent, 19 per cent, 27.8 per cent, 35 per cent, 41.3 per cent and 43 per cent – and those were just the ones I remembered. It all depended on whether you included state royalties, subtracted concessions, were talking about taxable income or tax actually paid, and which years you were talking about.

By allowing this kind of confusion to develop, the government gave credence to the idea that it didn't really know what it was talking about; that it had not, in the miners' words, thought it through. There were times, and this was one of them, when Rudd and his troops looked like a bunch of amateurs.

The only thing that saved them was that their opponents looked even sillier. The politically superfluous Julie Bishop did it again: Tony Abbott's loyal deputy committed a breach of security so absurd that even Greg Sheridan felt moved to attack her for embarrassing his first love, the spooks. Admittedly it was more a matter of ignorance than design: Bishop did not understand the difference between stealing a real identity and forging a fictitious one. The latter is indeed common practice throughout spookdom, but the former is considered unacceptable between allies, and Foreign Minister Stephen Smith really had no option but to react strongly against Israel's blatant abuse in giving the hit team who killed a Hamas arms dealer passports with the names of real Australians. But Bishop, even after receiving a confidential security briefing on the matter, stated publicly that Smith had overreacted and that, in any case, Australia did it too.

Bishop responded to inquiries about her very public gaffe by first denying that she had said it, then claiming to have misunderstood the very straightforward question, before finally casting doubt on the evidence against Mossad, which Australia's top police and intelligence agencies had found to be conclusive. Her performance transcended mere incompetence; it crossed the line into farce on the Barnaby Joyce level. It was not surprising that more than one government member accidentally referred to her as 'Bronwyn Bishop.' Abbott's front bench boasted not one, but two mad blondes. Let the jokes begin.

And just in case that wasn't distraction enough, Rudd announced that Australia would finally take Japan to the International Court of Justice in a bid to end 'scientific' whaling. But once again attention shifted to the other side as news broke that Malcolm Fraser had formally resigned from the Liberal Party last December, immediately after Tony Abbott became its leader. In fact the breach had been obvious for more than a decade. Fraser had put up with constant carping about his government from the left; this was only to be expected. But over the years his own party had joined in, calling his time in office the wasted years: he twice won landslide victories that included Senate majorities but failed to implement the radical neo-liberal program the right expected. The end came when his former lieutenant, John Howard, was elected as prime minister and not only continued the criticism but raised it to new heights. Fraser saw this as a deliberate act of treachery and replied in kind, thus endearing himself to his former sworn foes. The left was already coming around to him because of his charity work, environmentalism and anti-racist agenda, but it was the attacks on Howard that did the trick. The enemy of my enemy is my friend.

It is worth recalling just why Fraser was so hated in the first place. He came to power in the most ruthless manner possible, having undermined one leader (Harold Holt), destroyed two others (John Gorton and Billy Snedden) and then dragged the country to the brink of anarchy or even civil war with a series of outrageous and unprecedented breaches of convention. In government he was nice to whales, Aboriginals and (right-wing) Vietnamese asylum seekers, but persistently attacked the unions, public education and health; he effectively destroyed Whitlam's Medibank, which Hawke had to reinvent as Medicare. His best-known attempt at economic reform was the sale of the children's merry-go-round in Canberra. And even his supposed allies weren't immune from his malice: he dudded the mainly conservative premiers and gloated about it, and betrayed Margaret Thatcher over Zimbabwe. His private life wasn't too flash either: his overseas adventures led to a parliamentary question on notice (never answered) and culminated in him losing his trousers in Memphis. His idea of a joke was to load his fellow drinkers' coat pockets with pickled onions. And of course throughout his parliamentary career he was seen as a hardline right-winger, a radical conservative. So, if the squire of Nareen, the crazy grazier, found the extremism of Tony Abbott too horrible to tolerate, where did that leave the rest of us?

Well, at least some of us, and indeed a handful of his own party, tended towards Fraser's line. Abbott had unilaterally announced what amounted to Howard's policy on asylum seekers: temporary protection visas, off-shore processing, all the paraphernalia of the Pacific Solution. The corrupt economic basket case of Nauru instantly put up its withered hand and said, yes please, we're still bribable. But in the Liberal party room the usual suspects objected, Malcolm Turnbull said it wouldn't work and the public reception was less than enthusiastic; it might have played in 2001, but we had, as they say, moved on. The prospect of an election in which the perceived issue was which side could exhibit the most sadism towards boat people had lost its universal appeal. Liberal polling showed that it could still be effective in some places, but whether these places coincided with the marginals the party hoped to win was not immediately clear. Several Labor backbenchers reported that their constituents were worried about boat people, but Rudd stated with unaccustomed but welcome firmness that he would not try to outflank Abbott on the issue; he would not be part of a race to the bottom.

However, the next Newspoll suggested that, like it or not, that was how the public was seeing it. The primary votes of both major parties were down, with Labor collapsing to bedrock at 35 per cent. Dennis Shanahan triumphantly asserted that Labor could not win from that base; in fact the same poll showed Labor would have won narrowly, with a two-party-preferred total of 51.5 per cent. This relied on Labor gaining at least 80 per cent of the Green preferences, with the Greens running at a record 16 per cent. Bob Brown insisted that Labor should not rely on Green votes to get them across the line, but the Labor hardliners replied that no sane Green voter could possibly give preferences to Tony Abbott. But then, Labor hardliners believed that no sane person would vote Green in the first place, so the logic was not irresistible.

What the poll showed unequivocally was that while Labor was in deep doo-doo, the Coalition was not doing all that well either. The popularity of both leaders continued to fall; Rudd was down to a net minus eighteen with Abbott on minus twelve.

The only straw for the Labor people to cling to was that the figures for preferred prime minister were unchanged: Rudd led Abbott 49 to 33. The overall message was clear: a plague on both your houses, a fitting start to what promised to be a winter of political discontent. A mere three months earlier the voters had been in reasonably good spirits, preparing to re-elect a government which may have had its faults, but which still commanded trust and confidence, especially its leader. But through an extraordinary combination of political cowardice, panicky impetuousness and sheer bad judgment, that had all been pissed up against the wall. It now boiled down to a choice between the bad and the less bad, the suddenly unpalatable versus the still unthinkable. For a depressingly large part of the electorate, Informal was looking pretty good.

> *A Clock stopped—*
> *Not the Mantel's—*
> *Geneva's farthest skill*
> *Can't put the puppet bowing—*
> *That just now dangled still.*
> —EMILY DICKINSON

★ 10.

THE MINERS CELEBRATED the start of winter with a slap-up conference in Canberra, the one Kevin Rudd declined to attend pleading a previous engagement: the centenary of Andrew Fisher's Labor government. Instead he sent Martin Ferguson. Tony Abbott turned up to swear eternal loyalty, but had the grace to leave his carpet bag at the door. The miners had good reason to feel satisfied; they were drawing support from other sections of big business, and even Sir Rod Eddington, Rudd's personal business adviser, was making cautious noises in their favour. And last but not least, they were picking up the wavering elements among the public. The government could still claim that a majority agreed with the proposed tax, but it was drifting away.

The conference could report progress. But it could not report any real advances against the government. Rudd had some of the big executives in for pre-dinner drinks and what was later described as a frank exchange of views – in other words, a blazing row. He warned publicly that this was going to be a long hard fight, and added significantly that it could well go on until after the election. The political imperative remained: this time, don't back down. He and Wayne Swan in particular were taking it seriously; in parliament their indignation was rattling the windows. Abbott, of course, was matching them decibel for decibel. It was not the most enlightening of debates. And it appeared to be going nowhere, which made it a good time to get the hell out of it all.

I departed for Cairns, thence to cruise the Savannah Way to Darwin, camping as far from any news as possible. Forty days in the wilderness was, after all, a time-honoured way to clear the head. I could only afford thirty, but it still might do the job. Nothing in the so-called real world seemed to be working. But as it turned out, Cairns, although undoubtedly warmer, was no less depressing. Even in the deep north, it could not be denied that the government was in diabolical trouble. Not only did the banana benders not like Kevin Rudd's Great Big New Tax (54 per cent, according to the Galaxy poll), they didn't understand it (68 per cent said the government had explained it badly) and they didn't want to (anecdotal evidence). As a result, the Coalition was now clearly in front: 52 to 48 on two-party preferred.

The truly grim news was that Tony Abbott had caught up with Rudd in the preferred prime minister stakes, trailing by a single point: 44 to 45. Labor's fallback position had always been that their guy might be pretty much on the nose but the other guy was unelectable – too crazy to take seriously in the top job. The theory, now revealed as little more than wishful thinking, had been that, while the voters might find the idea of the Mad Monk a bit of a distraction, something to brighten up the daily spin-driven tedium that politics had become, when it came to casting a vote they would draw back; caution and discretion would take over. It now appeared that in Queensland

– Rudd's home state – the punters were preparing to forget about the parachute and jump out of the plane.

Admittedly this was Queensland, the state that gave us Joh Bjelke-Petersen, Russ Hinze, Clive Palmer and the cane toad. But where Queensland went, could Western Australia be far behind? And if the dominos started to fall, suddenly we would wake up to find Abbott in the Lodge, Joe Hockey in the Treasury, Julie Bishop running foreign policy, Philip Ruddock, Bronwyn Bishop and Kevin Andrews occupying ministries, and Barnaby Joyce – the shadow finance minister who had to take off his trousers to count up to twenty-one – naming his own price for keeping the Nationals in the Coalition. The prospect, once the stuff of febrile nightmare, was rapidly turning real. And the truly bad news was that no one in the Labor camp seemed to have a clue what to do about it.

Fortunately the unions were stepping up their own campaigning against both the miners and the Coalition. Labor was always going to use the line about Abbott planning to bring back WorkChoices as part of its scare campaign, and it was already having some subliminal effect. But it now looked as though the unions, realising that a change of government was suddenly a possibility, were going to get back on the airwaves in a big way. Frankly it was just as well; so far the government's advertising campaign extolling the RSPT had been even more boring and unconvincing than the miners' campaign against it – and given that all the facts and logic were on the government's side, that was condemnation indeed.

At least the backlash against Rudd's broken promise about ending political advertising had been less severe than might have been expected; Abbott and his colleagues had had a bit of fun with the apparent invocation of a national emergency, but by and large the public seemed to have shrugged it off. As Rudd and others pointed out, Howard did much worse and much more of it and in the current mood of disillusionment and despair at the whole process, that was all that needed to be said. All politicians are bastards, a politician is an arse upon which everything has sat except a man, and whoever you vote for, a politician always gets in, so why bother?

This public reversion to cynicism about politics and its place in society was perhaps the very worst legacy Rudd could leave Australia. His election campaign and the first year of his government did a lot to restore the hope and trust that Howard had so badly eroded; but in his last few months he pissed it all away in favour of timidity, indecision and, of course, a sack full of broken promises. Part of the problem was the group of time-servers, mercenaries and mug lairs he had collected around him; mainly refugees from the New South Wales right, they were ignorant of the past (it was irrelevant), uninformed about the present (they only talked to each other) and uninterested in the future (it didn't go past the next Newspoll). But it was Rudd himself who had been the most crashing disappointment: Kevin 07 had melted away into Kevin Zilch. What a pity Barack Obama had again been forced to cancel his visit; it would have been nice to see a politician who broke the mould and actually meant what he said, if only from a distance.

As the distances got greater, so did the sense of disconnection. News up around the Gulf of Carpentaria was sparse, which is probably why the somewhat eccentric Bob Katter has survived for so long as the local member, even after leaving the National Party to stand as a very independent Independent. And what did drift through had a touch of the surreal about it. It was, for example, disconcerting to learn belatedly that Kevin Rudd had been greeted in Perth by hordes of passionate demonstrators, outraged by the damage his proposed mining tax was going to do to their livelihood, their state and the Australian way of life. They were well organised, beautifully coordinated and most carried professionally printed placards embossed with well-crafted slogans, following identical patterns. A fine display of solidarity, which brought back ominous memories.

Some six decades ago a Labor prime minister was facing a political crisis of similar magnitude. In 1949, Ben Chifley went to an election on a platform of nationalising Australia's private banks. Again, there was well-organised outrage. Fred Daly, then a humble backbencher, used to tell the story of addressing a meeting in Sydney where ranks of well-dressed bank employees arrived to heckle him mercilessly. Exasperated, Fred accused one of them: 'I'll bet you're getting paid time and a half for this.' The indignant teller responded: 'That's a terrible lie. We're all on double time.' And the might of the banks eventually proved overwhelming. The High Court ruled their nationalisation unconstitutional and Labor lost the election anyway, ushering in twenty-three years of conservative rule.

The miners were no doubt hoping that history would repeat itself. Their financial clout was comparable to that of the banks, their rent-a-crowds equally well disciplined and, for the moment at least, it appeared that a decisive fraction of the electorate was persuaded that they, rather than the elected government, were the ones acting in the public interest. In the mining states of Western Australia and Queensland, Labor's polling was bleak, and elsewhere the mood was verging on panic. And at least some of the attack was coming from supposedly friendly quarters. Rudd's old mate Twiggy Forrest told the prime minister that this time the miners were serious, they were not bluffing. The tacit admission that in the past they may indeed have been crying wolf ought to have helped the government, but in fact it worked the other way; as with Tony Abbott, the statement that they did not always tell the truth was taken as evidence that this time they just might be.

Then a former Queensland treasurer, Keith de Lacy, now himself a mining executive, declared that Rudd had become an object of ridicule and should make way for someone who really cared about the country. The problem here was that de Lacey himself had long been an object of ridicule both inside and outside the Labor Party, and was in any case an enemy of Rudd dating back to the days when Rudd ran Premier Wayne Goss's office. No one had ever taken him seriously.

Far more damaging was David Marr and his *Quarterly Essay* concluding that there was anger at the core of Rudd, and that he was driven by rage. The implication many drew from this verdict, coming as it did from a friend, was that Rudd was not entirely rational, that perhaps, just perhaps, their trusted leader was turning into a bit of a psycho. Unwanted memories of Mark Latham came flooding back. Perhaps all Labor leaders came from the same distorted mould, and under a little pressure would crack.

This was not what Marr meant at all, and he said so loudly and publicly. I thought I understood what he was getting at: there was indeed anger in Rudd, a hatred of injustice which went back to his childhood and manifested itself in occasional temper tantrums but also in a reforming zeal, a passion for change which old Labor men and women referred to as the fire in his belly. There was absolutely nothing wrong with that, and indeed the major criticism of Rudd was that he did not have enough of it: he was the Ruddbot, programmed by self-control and spin. But in the circumstances it did not help. Abbott was supposed to be the erratic one, the wild man too risky to elect. If Rudd was also some kind of a loose cannon, what was the point of keeping him? After all, his reformist zeal didn't seem to have achieved all that much. Indeed, it seemed to consist largely of stumbling from one allegedly world-shattering crisis to another, with humiliating back-downs to punctuate the process. This, at least, was the view of the commentariat at News Limited.

But out in the real world, even in backblocks of Queensland, the reaction wasn't quite so clear-cut. I spent the Queen's Birthday weekend (Queensland still holds it) in the gulf country, where the punters were pouring in to the Normanton rodeo, and the miners of Mount Isa were congregating at Karumba for the fishing. If the pundits were right, this should have been the heartland of the revolt. But in fact the mood was more one of bewilderment than of betrayal. When they could be persuaded to talk about politics at all, which was not often, they said they felt that they really didn't understand Rudd, and that he didn't understand them either. He didn't talk to them and he didn't consult them; all they ever got was bumped-up little shiny-bums from the public service telling them what to do. There was anger and indignation, but most of it was aimed at the state government rather than the Feds, and there was an under-lying sense that if only Rudd could see what their problems were, he would do the right thing and they would trust him again. As for Tony Abbott – well, as one woman who described herself as being on the conservative side put it, he didn't seem to have the charisma to be prime minister. She probably meant gravitas rather than charisma, but the point was clear: Rudd might be a letdown, but the alternative was unconvincing. Labor's Plan A might still be in place, but only just. It was time – long past time, in fact – for Rudd to pull his finger out. At which point I passed into what Telstra routinely describes as the 3 per cent of Australia that gets no coverage of any kind whatsoever. It's a bloody big 3 per cent, let me tell you.

Being totally out of touch unfocuses the mind wonderfully; the day-to-day crises of the political scene fade into insignificance once they cease thrusting themselves upon what passes for one's attention. For ten days I was insulated from the media like a baby koala in its mother's pouch. No press, no radio, no phone, no internet. The blissful seclusion was broken just once, when I chanced across a copy of the *Northern Territory News* of Tuesday, 15 June. From this journal of record I learned that charter flights were bringing asylum seekers from Christmas Island to the mainland, which I had gleaned a month or so previously. This single piece of national news was buried under the comics. Apart from that, my sole contact with what the political pundits insist on calling the real world was campsite gossip.

In Lawn Hill someone mentioned that the press gallery appeared to have abandoned its febrile pursuit of a leadership change in the Labor Party; apparently it had finally dawned on even the ultimatum-threateners of the *Australian* that you can't have a challenge without a challenger. Instead, the gallery had reverted to its other favourite obsession: speculation about an election date. Someone else claimed to have heard an ABC news broadcast of Bob Brown gravely opining that although the election could be as late as April next year, it probably wouldn't be. Someone else noted that Barnaby Joyce had been reported as suggesting that the Coalition could win five, or possibly six, seats in Queensland. After that the conversation turned to regret that while the nearby fossil beds of Riversleigh had unearthed traces of the ancestry of every mammal currently living in Australia, the origins of Kevin Rudd and Tony Abbott remained a mystery. Of course, to retrace the ancestry of Barnaby Joyce, one would need to go further south, to the dinosaur fields of Richmond and Hughenden. And that was about it. For once my thoughts were unencumbered by knowledge, information, news, gossip, slander, innuendo, lies and the Murdoch press.

It must be said that in the far north, politics was not the main area of concern; the weather beat it every time. The flood-waters were receding, most roads were now open, and the countryside was alive with wattles, grevilleas, turkey bush and flowering gums, not to mention the odd roadside runner of wildflowers and the carpets of water lilies on the lagoons. On the rare occasions that people could be drawn into debate, they were anything but passionate.

Okay, so Kevin has been a bit of a disappointment, but weren't they all? At least most people kept their jobs through the global recession or whatever it was, and you had to give him a few marks for that. And as for all the talk about wasted money – well, we didn't get too much insulation out in the bush, but a few of the local schools have done all right out of the BER, whatever that is. And don't believe the miners are going to go broke: Century and Macarthur are doing very nicely thank you and don't let anyone tell you different.

One incredulous worker said he had heard stories that Gina bloody Rinehart, Lang bloody Hancock's daughter and the richest woman in the whole bloody country, was leading pro-tests. That'd be a bit of a joke wouldn't it? Another noted that the so-called protestors were adapting an old union chant: 'The miners, united, will never be defeated.' Give us a break. If the bosses want to pinch the workers' songs they could at least make up their own words. A few suggestions:

'The miners, tight-fisted, can never be resisted.'

'We're miners, we're heavy, we will not pay the levy.'

'The miners, hell-bent, refuse to pay the rent.'

'The miners have practice at dodging paying taxes.'

'Hey Kevin, piss off, it's our right to make huge profits.'

And so on *ad infinitum*. The overall feeling was that no one really understood how the new tax would work, but if the bosses were screaming so loudly, it couldn't be such a bad thing. This, of course, was precisely the reaction Kevin Rudd and Wayne Swan had been hoping for from the start.

The conventional wisdom is that apathy favours the incumbent, and that appeared to be the case in the outback. There was certainly space for Rudd to make a comeback; if he was able to divide the miners and reach some kind of agreement with even a few of them, it could be sold as a victory, and in the absence of anything much else would probably be enough to swing the balance. But it would take a mighty effort indeed in his second tem if he was ever to recapture that first fine, careless rapture of the heady days of Kevin 07. And Tony Abbott would need to mature considerably both as a person and a politician if he was to be given a second chance. In 2010 it appeared that we had escaped a double-dissolution election only to be saddled with a Double Disillusion. Hey, that's not a bad name for a book. In fact, it was the name of this one right up to the moment we got back into mobile-phone range on the morning of 24 June, to be greeted with the news that caucus was meeting to elect Julia Gillard as leader.

★

My first thought was that something utterly unexpected must have happened in the time I had been out of touch; but if it had, then surely some rumour of it would have reached us, even in the Never Never. But there had not been a hint in the Animal Bar at Karumba, among the fossils of Riversleigh, at the all-but-deserted roadhouse of Hell's Gate, at Heartbreak Hotel, at Bitter Springs, or even at Borroloola and Nitmiluk. If Rudd had really been caught *in flagrante delicto* with a goat, or worse still a Liberal, the bush telegraph had missed it. But then, with some relief, I caught up with the fact that just about everyone else was as stunned as I was. The switch had been made, quite literally, overnight. At least that journal of record, the *Northern Territory News*, was equal to the task. 'Julia set to be PM,' it announced boldly on Friday morning, pushing to the bottom of page one the real story: 'Shark meets the real JAWS,' with a photo of a large croc eating a shark. The juxtaposition was almost too good to be accidental; the only question was whether the coup in Canberra had been even more gory. And as the spin doctors moved in to mop up the blood, it was hard to see the justification for it.

Rudd's support had fallen a long way and Abbott was telling the troops he was within reach of a famous victory, but the polls appeared to be stabilising; indeed, if anything there were signs of a slight comeback. The war with the miners was raging, but concessions had been made and it seemed more likely than not that a truce would be called in the near future. Indeed, it was later revealed that Rudd and Twiggy Forrest had arrived at a potential peace deal, which was about to be put to the big boys at BHP Billiton and Rio Tinto. It might have needed the additional retreat to which Gillard later agreed, but the stalemate had been broken. The prospect was reasonably bright: Abbott would be forced to dismount from his tax tiger and the election would be fought on ground far more congenial to the government. Incumbent governments almost always picked up a few percentage points during the actual campaign and, as the experienced Bob McMullan pointed out, Labor was already back to a lead of 52 to 48 in Newspoll's two-party preferred and Rudd still led Abbott as preferred prime minister by seventeen points; no government had ever lost from that position so late in its first term.

It was true that the Essential poll showed that its constituents favoured dumping Rudd by a margin of 40 to 37, but the poll also favoured dumping Abbott, 47 to 29. There was absolutely no need to panic. Gillard had many attractive qualities that Rudd lacked but was untried at the top and had proved a bit flaky on policy, especially during the 2004 campaign. She was hardly a risk-free alternative. And surely she was at least nominally still involved with the left. What on earth were the right-wing powerbrokers doing supporting a basket-weaver?

Well, they later leaked that their own polling showed things were much more desperate than the public polls suggested: Labor was facing defeat and things were only getting worse; surely the swing of 25 per cent against Labor in the state by-election for Penrith proved it. Well, no; state elections were different and New South Wales was particularly different. It is possible that the warlords had the evidence they claimed, but they never actually produced it. Dennis Shanahan wrote one of his silliest pieces for the *Australian* explaining that everyone had misread Newspoll and that it really meant Labor under Rudd was unelectable; the two-party-preferred figure, the one his paper headlined, should be ignored in favour of – well, what? Dennis Shanahan's lifelong bias?

Tendentious as this was, it pointed to a growing trend. Rudd was to be expunged as quickly and quietly as possible, and the last two and a half years were to be treated as an unfortunate aberration. Sure, he might, as he himself listed in a lachrymose speech of farewell, have done a few good things – several actually – but that wasn't the point; he had been difficult and abrasive and he swore and he was rude to people, especially to the factional bosses. It was time to restore order.

Some years ago Philip Roth wrote a book which culminated in the assassination of a fictional – well, semi-fictional

– American president named Trick E. Dickson. The police had a lot of trouble with the case, not because it was hard to find suspects, but because it was too easy: every man, woman and dog was anxious to claim some of the credit. And thus it was with the political assassination of Kevin Rudd. Who could have guessed that there were so many killers lurking in the wings of Parliament House?

First up, of course, was Tony Abbott; he had a scalp, and a major one it was. He was joined on stage by those who had installed him in his own position: Nick Minchin, who led while Eric could only Abet, and the rest of the push who knifed Malcolm Turnbull. Then there were the miners, who had spent about $7 million in bankrolling the job, and there was plenty more where that came from if the new prime minister wouldn't play ball. But none of these could have succeeded without the pollsters, a bizarre cult whose rise to prominence was paralleled only by that of their fellow witchdoctors, the economists. And of course there were the media, most notably the hit-men and women of the Murdoch press, whose relentless campaign eventually turned their endless predictions of Rudd's downfall into a self-fulfilling prophecy. The *Australian* gave its own team, particularly Dennis Shanahan and Peter van Onselen, top marks in this regard. Inevitably the faction leaders played their role, as did loud-mouthed unionists like Paul Howes, who announced to the world that his withdrawal of support meant Rudd was finished. And we could not leave out Julia Gillard herself: in the end there had to be a candidate, and when the time was right she made herself available.

But it was Labor's parliamentary caucus that pulled the trigger. Rudd insisted that he had been elected by the Australian people, and in the broad sense that was true: the last election was all about Kevin 07. But it was only the electors of Griffith who voted for him personally; it was the vote of the caucus that gave him the leadership, and what the caucus gives it can take away. True, the manner of the execution was as ruthless as it was unexpected: Gillard's loyalty persevered to the last minute, and might have lasted beyond that had it not been for the public revelation that Rudd's chief minder, Alister Jordan, was testing it out. Jordan and Rudd's other whiz-kid, Lachlan Harris, were among the few not to claim credit for their boss's decease, but they were being overly modest. Their arrogance and thuggery, their ignorance and scorn of Labor history, tradition and processes did as much to isolate Rudd from his colleagues inside and outside parliament and to turn a potentially friendly press gallery into enemies as had Rudd's own abrasiveness and his monomaniac belief that he could do it all himself.

And it was this, of course, that finally brought things to a head. The Australian Labor Party is a collective, formed as a huge political union and embodying the union ideals of equality, mutual loyalty and mateship. It will tolerate and even welcome strong leaders, but there are certain rituals which must be observed. One is to show respect to the tribal elders, however bumptious and unpleasant they may be. One line Rudd's critics used to justify his destruction was: 'The people have stopped listening to him.' But a couple of weeks earlier, Mark Arbib, the godfather of what Tony Abbott picturesquely described as 'the Sussex Street death squad,' had seen the problem rather differently: 'He's stopped listening to me.'

Actually he hadn't, or if he had it was only recently. It was Arbib and his mates from the New South Wales right, backed by Swan and Gillard, who had persuaded Rudd to drop the ETS – the root cause of his troubles. And it was clear Arbib still saw himself as the master, the fount of all political wisdom. It was a remark worthy of his former New South Wales colleagues, the much-loathed Eddie Obeid and Joe Tripodi; comparisons with the revolving door of that state's leadership became unavoidable, and Julia Gillard was forced to emulate the embattled premier Kristina Kenneally by declaring herself nobody's puppet. Following Arbib there were others who felt equally snubbed and they had no trouble mobilising resentment among the lesser figures who had never enjoyed privileged access in the first place. Thus the scene was set.

The speed of the execution was indeed unprecedented, but the circumstances were not. Rudd was a prime minister deposed by his party after winning just one election and in his first term in office; and so was John Gorton when cut down to make way for Billy McMahon in 1971. In both cases the party's powerbrokers felt that their own base was threatened by the leader's unorthodox behaviour, his failure to consult and his willingness to ignore time-honoured (some would say hidebound) procedures. They felt that they needed to return to a safe, traditional leader who would follow their rule-book. But not only did they pick a dud in McMahon, they elected Gorton as his deputy, a handicap too great for any leader to bear. It is a memory Gillard no doubt kept in mind when she was considering a role for Rudd in her government. As it turned out, she decided against any role: Rudd remained on a promise if the government was returned, and that was it. But the family was not entirely out of it. Daughter Jessica had a book ready for publication which, incredibly, concerned the overthrow of an idealistic Labor prime minister by his more determined female deputy. And nephew Van Thanh Rudd was lining up to stand for the Revolutionary Socialist Party against Gillard in her seat of Lalor. Rudd had at least one other loyal ally (apart from the ever-faithful Jasper and Abby). A bewildered Barack Obama rang the man he had once described as sharing his own world view more closely than any other leader before making the ritual congratulatory call to his successor. The prophet was not without honour, save in his own caucus.

Even there, Gillard's ascension was not universally accepted. The fringe reluctance was pointed up by the declaration of Lindsay Tanner, who in a better world would have been prime minister himself, that he was quitting politics. Tanner said he had planned to do so anyway, but the fact remained that he had been a long-time political foe of Gillard and, unlike his factional colleague Kim Carr, had not come around to accepting her. In their days in student politics he had talked of her being opportunistic and untrustworthy, and his opinion had never really changed. The pair had worked together in Rudd's kitchen cabinet, but Tanner had never been prepared to work under her as prime minister. Indeed, he had told colleagues she would replace Rudd only over his dead body, and now he kept his word.

Ostensibly the caucus locked itself in behind Gillard, as it had to. But there were many who were unhappy about the manner of Rudd's removal, if not the fact of it, and, as Rudd had recently pointed out to the miners, the Labor Party has a long memory. The caucus members were not the only ones with lingering doubts; among the general public the doubts were loud and persistent. Letter-writers bewailed the fact that Gillard had finally proved disloyal to her leader and allowed herself to be used as a Trojan horse by the Neanderthals of the right. Interestingly, much of the most passionate condemnation came from Gillard's own gender; three leftish women of my acquaintance swore they would never vote Labor again. Did this mean they would vote for Tony Abbott? No, there were limits, but they would give their first preference to the Greens or independents – anyone but the party that had betrayed its own prime minister. One lamented that, as a feminist and a Labor supporter, she had really been looking forward to voting for Gillard as prime minister, but now she was giving up politics altogether and planned to vote informal. Rudd's dismissal marked the end of the Australian Labor Party as she knew it. And to cap it all, Phillip Adams announced that he was resigning from the party. Given that the party had resigned from Phillip Adams some years previously, this caused less of a stir than he had perhaps hoped.

Tony Abbott, too, had a piece of history to contemplate. The last Liberal leader to claim the scalp of a prime minister in office was John Hewson, whose Fightback! package provided the opportunity for Paul Keating to bushwhack Bob Hawke. Abbott was working for Hewson at the time and saw the triumph crumble to disaster. Every silver lining has a cloud. Actually the Labor meltdown produced quite a big cloud for Abbott, who had finally developed something of a positive program for government. Now his twelve-point plan was enveloped in the miasma of the changeover. And his promise of a big revamp for mental health (an area Labor had been accused of ignoring in its own health reforms) didn't fare much better, in spite of a good reception from professionals in the field, including Australian of the Year Patrick McGorry. Eventually he decided to play it safe and go back to being photographed in athletic poses with children until the dust settled.

At the same time we witnessed a series of forays into the life and habits of Gillard's partner, Tim Mathieson, who had until now been an innocent bystander, outside the hunters' spotlight. Mathieson was explicitly or implicitly accused of uncontrollable satyriasis, closet homosexuality and being a token male handbag employed to cover up Gillard's own deviant tendencies. The magazines, the internet and the sleazier pubs were alive with the sound of bullshit. Combined with Gillard's admission of atheism, it fuelled the conservatives who wanted to portray her ascension to the prime ministership as a Bridge Too Far, as Kevin Rudd might once have put it.

Rudd, incidentally, was belatedly getting support from unexpected quarters. Greg Sheridan in the *Australian* said Gillard should have appointed him immediately as foreign minister, no ifs, no buts, no mucking around. Noel Pearson suggested that Rudd was ideally placed to continue and complete the task of reconciling black and white Australia. Malcolm Turnbull wrote a piece conflating the former prime minister with Shakespeare's Coriolanus and W.B. Yeats. The man himself, meanwhile, had returned to Queensland but had boarded Jasper and Abby with friends. Under the circumstances, this was seen as further evidence of emotional instability.

All this and an election to follow. Clearly the contest would be unique: it seemed to be turning into some kind of political revue. Over a long lunch some of us started playing with titles for the closing number: 'The Spunk and the Monk,' 'The Oxford Blue and the Red Menace,' 'Better a Redhead than a Deadhead.' And it looked as if a title would be needed pretty soon. While some pundits (mostly the ones barracking for Abbott) were urging Gillard to delay, to give herself time to get established as the incumbent in her own right before submitting her government to the people, the majority wanted to get the show on the road. The polls had not bounced quite as much as some had expected, but there was a definite shift back to Labor from the swingers on both the left and the right. It might or might not last, so grab it while you've got the chance.

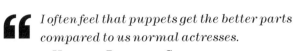 *I often feel that puppets get the better parts compared to us normal actresses.*
—HELENA BONHAM CARTER

★ 11.

JULIA EILEEN GILLARD had begun 2010 as acting prime minister. Her deal with Kevin Rudd, which assured the defeat of Kim Beazley and the ascension of the duumvirate, had always assumed that Rudd would serve two terms before any thought of a handover – and Gillard was content to wait. This did not mean that she was not ambitious, or that she did not regard the top job as her eventual due; after all, she had contributed more votes to the coup than had Rudd. The right was split between Rudd and Beazley, but the left – or at least most of it – was solid for Gillard. Some of the left's key players had their reservations: Kim Carr and Lindsay Tanner had both clashed with Gillard earlier in her career and still viewed her with a certain amount of suspicion. But she was undeniably the most popular figure in the caucus, even if the caucus as a whole was not quite ready for a leader still nominally aligned to the left.

But this changed with the weakening of the factions and Gillard's embrace of the centre; by the end of Labor's second year in office, Gillard was universally accepted as the heir apparent, not only within the party but by the wider public.

Incredibly, the right-wing commentators joined in the general approbation. Andrew Bolt confessed that he was smitten and Janet Albrechtsen immediately moved to make it a threesome. Even Alan Jones, not normally attracted to either Labor or women, succumbed. And of course Australia's feminists could hardly wait to see one of their own in the Lodge. All the signs were that the succession, when it came, would be a smooth and seamless one. Equally, the signs were that it would not come for a while yet.

While she waited, Gillard was getting plenty of practice. Rudd's partiality for overseas travel, together with his infrequent holidays, meant that Gillard's home in the Melbourne suburb of Altona was often the seat of government. It was probably more comfortable than the seaside caravan from which Doug Anthony would run the country in Malcolm Fraser's absence, but it was still pretty informal. Altogether, before her ascension, Julia Gillard acted as prime minister on 227 separate occasions, covering a total of 185 days. She signed off on some 2480 documents. It wasn't a bad record, but it wasn't the real thing. While Kevin Rudd was conscious, which seemed to be nearly twenty-four hours a day, he was involved. Even from 16,000 kilometres away, you knew he was straining to pay attention to every detail of what he clearly considered to be *his* government. And despite what his minders pretended, he was never really on holiday; he was always riffling and shuffling away somewhere, his stubby finger pointed to resume control in an instant. Being Rudd's deputy was a lot better than being a common or garden minister – most of them never got to do anything much, other than attempt to meet the often impossible demands Rudd imposed on them. But it remained just a dress rehearsal. No one could have guessed that the opening night would come so quickly.

But it did, and the Prima Donna set a lot of precedents. She, of course, became Australia's first woman prime minister. She also became Australia's first unmarried prime minister. Many of Australia's twenty-six male prime ministers had very rocky marriages, unions which would certainly have been terminated (or, in at least one case, not entered into at all) were it not for the perceived need to have an officially sanctioned partner. Gillard had the partner but not the official sanction; she was in the state that strict Christians refer to as 'living in sin.' This did not worry her as she was an avowed atheist – another first. Among her predecessors, Gough Whitlam described himself as 'a fellow traveller' with Christianity and Bob Hawke claimed to be an agnostic, but no one before Gillard had taken the final step.

Even if she had stuck to her first factional alliance, she would not be the first leftie – James Scullin and John Curtin were far more radical – nor the first foreigner: Chris Watson was born in Chile. Indeed, she was not even the first from Wales: that title belongs to Billy Hughes, hardly one of Labor's favourite role models. But she was probably the first redhead and certainly the first to come from a district known as The Valley of the Witch. That record seems destined to stand for a very long time. So a Gillard prime ministership had novelty value. The question facing the voters in the bleak mid-winter during which she called the election was: What else did it have? Or indeed, what else would it have if it were allowed to continue?

It was an unexpected and unwelcome dilemma. Most people felt that they did not even know Kevin Rudd yet; they had barely started coming to terms with one prime minister and now they were confronted with another one altogether. And they had not really got used to the new Opposition leader either. Australian politics was not meant to be like this. Give us a break.

The first couple of weeks gave little indication of the choice the voters were now facing. Gillard seemed more intent on proving that she was not Kevin Rudd than in defining her own directions. And her past was equally vague. Her reputation as a firebrand of the left was, it turned out, more an invention of the Opposition than a true history. Even in her student days she made her reputation not by storming the barricades but by wresting control of the student union away from the Maoists and Trots, who devoted their time and resources to international crusades on behalf of the Palestinians; she concentrated instead on more parochial matters such as student welfare. Nonetheless she joined Labor's left faction, although its leading figures such as Tanner and Carr suspected this was more in an attempt to gain preselection than through ideological conviction – in those days the terms left and right still meant something. That she eventually secured the ultra-safe electorate of Lalor despite their objections was a tribute to her toughness and determination. From then on it was a steady and relentless rise.

Gillard supported Simon Crean's leadership, and when he lost it, she switched to Mark Latham, quickly becoming a key figure and confidante. The bold but impractical idea of Medicare Gold – free health and hospital care for all senior citizens – was her first major attempt at policy formulation, and although it ultimately failed it marked her as a serious player. When Latham self-destructed, Gillard remained loyal; almost alone among his former colleagues, she refrained from bagging him in public. And for more than three years she showed the same loyalty to Kevin Rudd. At first their political marriage appeared to be no more than a union of convenience between a basically incompatible pair. But the odd couple proved a successful and productive partnership: Gillard successfully dismantled WorkChoices (although not to quite the extent the trade unions demanded) and steered through two major education reforms – the national curriculum and the MySchool website – against considerable opposition, most of which came from the left and in particular the teachers' unions, an important part of Labor's support base. While the right applauded, the left saw it as a betrayal. If she had ever been a true believer, she was one no longer.

In the end it was the much-reviled right, led by the Mafiosi from New South Wales, who raised the great red hope of the Victorian left to the top. The Victorian left maintained its traditional role as a losing minority by supporting Kevin Rudd.

Having given exclusive first interviews to almost everyone, Gillard's first move as prime minister was to de-Ruddify the government by clearing up some of the problem areas. There was an immediate announcement that the title, though not the function, of Tony Burke's portfolio would be changed: henceforth he would be known as the minister for sustainable population, the new adjective signalling Gillard's rejection of Rudd's controversial espousal of a Big Australia.

And then to the big one: the Resource Super Profits Tax, to be re-labelled as the friendlier Minerals Resource Rent Tax. Gillard had already brokered a truce in the advertising war and sent Wayne Swan and the underrated resources minister Martin Ferguson to negotiate the terms of surrender. Swan was the hard cop; as one of the big success stories of the government's first term, he was not always liked but was universally respected. And good old Marn Fersn spoke the miners' language and empathised with their aims. They made a good team and were given *carte blanche*: the imperative now was not to hold their ground but to make peace at any cost.

And of course they did. The Labor Party made Julia Gillard

leader because it thought it was in trouble and it needed a troubleshooter, a fixer; and now she delivered. The first fix was in and the big miners were off the government's back. The small miners weren't too happy about it but they were never the problem; it was BHP Billiton, Rio Tinto and Xstrata, with the backing of the Minerals Council of Australia, who were running the advertising campaign. That now stopped, and Ms Fixit took all the credit. Actually, Kevin Rudd and his old mate Twiggy Forrest (who was also miffed at being left out of the final champagne-cracking) had done most of the work; Gillard's role was to make the final capitulation, a lowering of the tax rate from the previously untouchable 40 per cent to a headline 30 per cent, which, when the other concessions were taken in, falls to 22.5 per cent – just over half the original proposal. But the result, if you believed the Treasury figures (and Tony Abbott was not the only one who thought they were a bit too good to be true), was that the big boys would still be paying $10.5 billion in the first two years, a sum they would not have paid otherwise. As fixes went, it wasn't too bad.

Of course, there were other changes. The government dropped its offer to pick up 40 per cent of establishment costs, the threshold at which the tax came in was effectively doubled and the only mines affected were those producing coal and iron ore; for all other minerals, including bauxite and aluminium, it would be business as usual. This was not as big a cop-out as it sounded because these commodities had not seen the huge price rises and consequent windfall gains in profits that had made coal and iron ore such bonanzas; should the same thing happen to them, there would no doubt be moves to bring them into the new system. So it wasn't the neat, inclusive policy package that Rudd, Swan and Ken Henry had envisaged; but at this stage of the electoral cycle, it didn't need to be. And it left the

Opposition out on a limb. Tony Abbott, in a rare attack of consistency, stood his ground: it was still a great big new tax and he'd abolish it and the election would be a referendum on tax, he cried. But it quite clearly wouldn't – the issue was dead.

Gillard now turned her attention to the next problem area, asylum seekers, where the outlook was less happy. She had already been talking tough. The anxieties of insecure voters in the crowded western suburbs of Sydney were, she said, very real and must be addressed. Sure they were very real, but that did not mean they were either sensible or necessary. As had been pointed out countless times, boat people made up a minuscule proportion of Australia's net migration and, in international terms, their numbers were insignificant. The suggestion that they constituted some sort of threat to Australia and our way of life was not a legitimate anxiety but rampant paranoia, fuelled by racist bigots and opportunistic politicians.

The proper way – the Labor way – to deal with such worries was simply to give the facts; the truth was that there were no grounds for concern, and the prime minister should have taken the leading role in explaining this. But that was too difficult and would take too long; it was a policy, not a fix. So Gillard instead called for a full and open debate – well, at least for a day or so, until she was ready to announce her deeply considered solution. Say what you really feel, she urged. Abandon all thought of political correctness. And while you're at it, abandon reason, compassion, humanity, decency and any consideration of Australia's international obligations and reputation. Let it all hang out.

Responding enthusiastically, the Opposition spokesman Scott Morrison, already committed to reintroducing the brutal policies of the Howard government, went still further: any asylum seekers without valid identity documents (something of a luxury when fleeing persecution through the medium of people smugglers) would not be considered for processing. Final assessments would be made not by the officials who did the processing but by faceless bureaucrats elsewhere. Well, they wouldn't be final; the minister – Morrison – would retain the power of veto. He did not go so far as to say that those who received the thumbs-down would have their fingernails removed with red-hot pincers, but he left the option open. Nothing was too sadistic to contemplate. In the circumstances Gillard had plenty of room to move; all she needed to do was to produce a policy marginally less horrible, and the left would have to cling to Labor as the least worst option. But there was plenty of room to placate the anxious Westies, so she did. Kevin Rudd's prediction of the lurch to the right the party's warlords were demanding had come true.

Gillard's speech at the Lowy Institute contained a moment of hope: she deplored the course the now decade-old debate had taken and reminded everyone that even if all the boat people proved to be genuine refugees, they would make up just 1.6 per cent of Australia's total immigration. But instead of suggesting that we all calm down and stop worrying about an intake which would take twenty years to fill the Melbourne Cricket Ground, she proposed her own complex and hideously expensive version of off-shore processing: a purpose-built centre on East Timor. This, she insisted, was not another Pacific Solution; it wasn't even an Arafura Sea solution. It was a regional solution, and she had already rung New Zealand about it. Also the United Nations High Commissioner for Refugees and the East Timor president, José Ramos-Horta, and none of them had dismissed the idea out of hand.

True, but none had scrambled on board either. Tony Abbott made the obvious point that Ramos-Horta was the wrong man: he was merely the ceremonial head of state, not the government.

His role was rather more than ceremonial but the criticism was a valid one; it looked as if Gillard, in her haste for a headline, had blundered. Ramos-Horta said he'd talk to the prime minister, Xanana Gusmão, but when interviewed, Gusmão had reservations. He wasn't the only one: the vice-president, José Luís Guterres, said an agreement was most unlikely. The opposition Fretilin party opposed the idea out of hand and then the parliament, including Gusmão's own supporters, voted unanimously against it. In case Canberra hadn't noticed, in a couple of days they repeated the exercise. Gillard, having first denied that she had singled Timor out as her preferred site, now said bravely that negotiations with Ramos-Horta (who had been flicked the whole issue by Gusmão) were continuing, but that was about it. It appeared that Gillard's obsession with finding the political fix had overwhelmed the need for a viable policy. Abbott brushed the whole thing aside, insisting that only he had the policies to save Australia – from what he did not make clear. The debate, if it could be called that, vanished into a cesspool of name-calling and abuse.

This was a pity because a regional processing centre for asylum seekers, based in a country which is a signatory to the United Nations' convention on refugees and run by, or at least under the auspices of, the United Nations High Commissioner for Refugees, was actually not a bad idea. It would remove the need for makeshift UNHCR offices throughout the region and end the perception that some applicants in some places received preferential treatment. And it would kill off the people-smuggling rackets; if all asylum seekers had to go through the same gate, wherever they came from or however they arrived, there would be no advantage in risking the desperate and perilous journey by boat. The camps in places like Indonesia and Malaysia would not be emptied overnight, but an orderly system could be set up whereby they would be filtered through the single processing centre as opportunities for resettlement became available. Countries willing to accept successful applicants could cooperate on quotas and plan ahead to make ready the necessary facilities. Altogether a win–win situation.

And where to put the centre? That was a no-brainer. Obviously the biggest and richest country in the region, the one that would pay most of the cost anyway: Australia. This, of course, was where the logic broke down. The whole point of Julia Gillard's proposal was to keep the bastards out – offshore processing. The official explanation was that they could not be allowed in because that would give them access to the Australian legal system and the possibility of justice, clearly an unthinkable concept in the current climate. But the real reason was much simpler: the anxious voters of Lindsay wouldn't like it. And this did not mean that they were racists or rednecks; good heavens, no. What it did mean was that they were extremely ill-informed, and it would be too much trouble for sensible and decent people to persuade them otherwise. So we would step aside and allow the real racists and rednecks to win the debate by default. But by golly, we would look tough while we were doing it. The picture of Julia Gillard and the local member, David Bradbury, dolled up in flak jackets on a patrol boat in Darwin Harbour, visited for that sole purpose, surely ranked as one of the silliest and most depressing of the year to date.

To get back to the story: having rejected the largest and richest country in the region as the preferred site, where should we look next? Well, obviously to the smallest and poorest, or at least a close contender for the position. Timor-Leste was a horribly cynical choice; it still would have been even if the negotiations had been sensibly handled and the government and populace had shown themselves willing. But since they were clearly opposed, and any future consultation would have to take the form of bullying and bribery, the whole proposal was nothing more than an ugly and brutal political fix, and a seriously botched one at that – a sort of stuffed-up version of whatever-it-takes. It might or might not get Gillard through to the election, but it will give her, and the rest of us, an awful hangover on the morning after.

And what do you take for an awful hangover? One recipe is a raw egg, which was what one disgruntled punter threw at the prime minister during a visit to Perth. Her response was commendably mild, especially when compared to one of her predecessors. When someone threw an egg at Billy Hughes at Warwick in 1917, he retaliated by setting up the Commonwealth police. But Gillard's restraint could not hide the fact that her ascension to the job was causing divisions in the community; a Morgan poll found that although Labor held a comfortable 55–45 lead on the two-party-preferred vote, the electorate was split along gender lines. Women preferred Gillard over Abbott by a ratio of 60–40, but men were divided 50–50. The situation was fluid.

And the distractions continued. No less than three reports were released condemning Labor's failed Green Loans scheme, necessitating still more patching up. The good news was the economy: another fall in the unemployment figures, although even this had its drawbacks – it could lead to another interest-rate rise in the middle of the election campaign. Unambiguously good was a big jump in export earnings, which could mean that the government would have an extra couple of billion to play with once the election was announced. The betting was now overwhelmingly on an August poll date, with the general feeling that as soon as Gillard could come up with her final quick fix on climate change, she would be off to Yarralumla. In anticipation, Stephen Conroy announced a new roll-out of national broadband to cover the marginal seats on the New South Wales north coast, and also a postponement of his unpopular plan to censor the internet for the foreseeable future. The decks were cleared, the hatches battened down. All that remained was for either or both of the major parties to come up with a credible platform. As things were, the only leader who appeared even half-way rational was the Greens' Bob Brown. But he didn't have to worry about seats like Lindsay.

The Nielsen poll of 12 July noted that Labor's primary vote had settled back to 39 per cent, with the two-party-preferred on 52 per cent and Gillard leading Abbott as preferred PM by 56 to 35. It wasn't quite the boost the numbers men had been hoping for – after all, the bottom line of 52–48 was precisely what Newspoll had shown on the eve of the killing off of Kevin Rudd – but it would provide a very satisfactory platform for the start of a campaign. Even the professionally dour John Faulkner allowed himself a hint of a smile when questioned about it. Somewhat reluctantly the senator had agreed to join her on the campaign trail as guide and confidant, a function he had performed for three former leaders: Kim Beazley, Mark Latham and Kevin Rudd. It would give him a chance to bring his success rate to 50 per cent.

All tribes need their elders, and the Labor tribe needs them more than most. The party depends on its history and tradition and the continuity the elders give its day-to-day operations. Although the ALP calls itself a progressive party, it is often reluctant to embrace change, and it only does so when the new directions get the imprimatur of those seen as the real guardians of the party's soul. Thus the departure of three of the party's most revered figures at the next election would be a critical event. Julia Gillard saw the problem and was able to persuade Faulkner, the most esteemed of them and a man widely regarded as the repository of Labor's true beliefs and traditions, to hang around for a bit longer, albeit as a backbencher rather than a senior minister. But Bob McMullan, snubbed by Kevin Rudd in spite of being the most experienced of all of them, and Lindsay Tanner, once himself a real leadership prospect, were out of the place. Apart from Faulkner, this left only Simon Crean and Kim Carr as survivors from a previous Labor era; both have proved their ability and both are steeped in Labor lore, but neither commands the respect given unstintingly to Faulkner by all the factions.

It should not be forgotten that when Paul Keating lost the 1996 election, Faulkner was Gough Whitlam's choice as his successor; Whitlam's idea was that the party should install an interim leader until a seat in the House of Representatives could be found for the New South Wales senator. This was, of course, fantasy; apart from Kim Beazley's obvious qualifications for the job, the party was not yet ready to give the leadership to a figure from the left. But it is a measure of Faulkner's standing that it could even be discussed. Whitlam, of course, like all Labor's former leaders, is a tribal elder himself, but his retirement from parliament means that he can only figure as a distant commentator. Bob Hawke, Paul Keating, Kim Beazley and even Mark Latham frequently perform a similar task and it is a useful one, but the caucus needs resident elders of its own. Crean, Carr and Faulkner are there to fill the roles; after a decent interval Kevin Rudd, if he perseveres in parliament, will no doubt join them.

That will make four people who are still serious about policy rather than just polling. As we used to say about Anzac Day parades, the ranks are thinner but the faces are still proud. And the party marches on. Moving forward, Gillard assured us – interminably. Perhaps we should have been grateful; Kevin

Rudd probably would have said advancing with directional positivity.

Tony Abbott, of course, had his own slogans: real action, direct action. Unfortunately, that was exactly what his colleagues were doing in Queensland, where the Liberal–National Party executive had already axed three of its federal candidates and was looking askance at two others. Both sides agreed that Queensland was the vital, frontline state. Abbott said bluntly that it was where the election would be won and lost, with ten marginal seats in play. And the axing of hometown boy Kevin Rudd should have given the Coalition a head start. Internal party brawling now looked like nullifying the advantage, and it was even revealed that in the case of Michael Johnson in Ryan, the cops had been called in. Abbott was spending a lot of time in the Sunshine State, where he was apparently well received, but this would not mean a lot if his candidates were busily making themselves unelectable. He also had his worries in New South Wales, where the Liberals' state leader, Barry O'Farrell, had inadvertently made public a tweet referring to Gillard as 'the ranga' and revealing that the Libs were having trouble finding credible candidates to stand in Sydney's western suburbs, the other key area replete with marginals. On the other hand he would have been encouraged by a bumper sticker reading: 'Don't let Julia stool ya.' Its meaning may not have been entirely clear, but it was obviously uncomplimentary to the prime minister.

Gillard, meanwhile, relaxed by launching the second volume of Blanche d'Alpuget's bedside biography of her husband who, Gillard announced, was her idol and role model. Bob Hawke agreed; he was his own idol and role model too, and he would be delighted to join her election campaign. The book provoked a furious reaction from Paul Keating, who said it was all wrong and more importantly had failed to give him the credit for everything. This febrile clashing of ageing egos was a momentary distraction from the fact that Gillard had still not announced her fix for climate change, which was generally seen as the last obstacle to the calling of the now inevitable August election.

And then, on Saturday 17 July, the fifty-fifth anniversary of the opening of Disneyland, she made the pilgrimage to Yarralumla. Gillard had taken the plunge, but we were left wondering: what exactly (or even approximately) was the election about? The easy answer was that it was, as Gillard sonorously proclaimed, our birthright; she would not really be prime minister until she was elected to the job by the people. As well as displaying a woeful ignorance of the Westminster system, this was unsatisfactory because we still had no idea what we were being asked to vote for. This was the first election in living memory to be called without either side of politics having produced a single serious policy.

Sure, Tony Abbott had made noises about spending money on mental health and taxing business to pay for parental leave, but apart from that it was a simple and meaningless slogan: Real Action, Direct Action. Gillard was even vaguer: sustainable population, regional centre for asylum seekers, but above all moving forward – again and again and again. Presumably the next few weeks would see some clarification, but at first glance it appeared that we were to be asked to vote not on matters of policy but on impressions of personality. Labor was telling us that Abbott was dangerous, risky and not to be trusted; the Coalition was telling us that Gillard was incompetent, opportunistic and treacherous. Such was the state of political discourse in the Lucky Country.

We had received a taste of just how intellectually vacuous the campaign was likely to be when the prime minister gave what was billed as a major address on the economy at the

National Press Club on the Thursday before her trip to Yarra-lumla. It was certainly not major; in the real world it would have struggled to make lance-corporal. After half an hour of reassuring clichés Gillard was ready for questions, and after a few predictably innocuous sallies, which she batted aside, the ponderous form of Laurie Oakes lumbered to his feet. For a wonderful moment we imagined that the doyen might break the mould and say something like: 'Okay, Ms Gillard, that's enough of the bullshit. Let's get down to the nitty-gritty. All together now ...' – and the press gallery would rise as one and chant in unison – 'Julia! Show us your ... vision. Or show us your ... policies. Or at least show us your ...' But alas, it was not to be. Instead we got a story about how the execution of Kevin Rudd was even nastier than it had first appeared, with Gillard apparently breaking an agreement. It was an important foot-note to history, and the polls showed that the swingers were understandably concerned about the manner in which the party had dumped its prime minister, although whether this would actually be a vote-changer in five weeks' time was highly doubtful. But the grim fact was that this was the headline story from the event because Gillard herself had given the hacks nothing worth writing about. Politics 101 would suggest that when you were about to call an election, it would be wise to have something to say. It did not augur well.

There were two straws left to cling to. One was climate change. Gillard was widely expected to announce a climate change fix (not policy) before calling the election, in the same way as she had announced supposed fixes for the mining tax and asylum seekers. The fact that she hadn't suggested that this time the easy, populist approach might have been rejected and perhaps, just perhaps, we would get something a bit more thoughtful and effective. And the other was that in spite of the very careful control Gillard has exhibited since 24 June and before it, it was obvious that she had a genuine commitment to education. At least this was a good Labor tradition: Kim Beazley always wanted to become the education prime minister and Kevin Rudd made an education revolution the centrepiece of his own campaign. Gillard had been something of a reformer in the portfolio and might yet surprise us.

The only other subject at the Press Club which brought any signs of enthusiasm was when she was asked about the latest spat between Bob Hawke and Paul Keating; she admitted she was enjoying it. Well, weren't we all, but it contained its own warning signs. The hard operators in the party were now urging her to forget her promise to find Kevin Rudd a senior ministerial job after the election, predicting that to do so would produce another bitter and messy feud, this time not in the gossip columns but in the cabinet room. Hawke had the grace to retire after Keating displaced him, and Rudd should be forced to do the same. They also blamed Rudd for Oakes's story, but this was specious. Both Gillard and Rudd had reported on the crucial meeting to their supporters, which meant that the story had gained wide currency within the party and beyond. It was true that Rudd had form on talking to Oakes, but so did any number of politicians, including Gillard. And in public, Rudd had behaved impeccably. He had pursued his interests and contacts in Washington, but he could hardly be blamed for that – although of course he had been, by the usual suspects. He remained a problem but he was hardly the most urgent one. First Gillard had to be elected, and to do that she had to give us reasons to vote for her. An endorsement from Cassandra, the *Sydney Morning Herald*'s answer to Paul the psychic German octopus, was hardly sufficient.

> **There are many advantages in puppets.**
> **They never argue. They have no crude views...**
> **They have no private lives.** —OSCAR WILDE

★ 12.

WE WERE OFF AND RUNNING – or at least some of us were. In spite of Abbott boasting that he was ready for an election at any time, it took several days to get the Liberal Party headquarters set up. Not an auspicious start. He did, however, promise us a dirty, filthy election campaign, but only from the Labor side, of course. Gillard, sticking to the message, promised nothing and Wayne Swan said that it would be an austere sort of campaign with no big spending. And there would be five weeks of it. Oh dear.

The situation was fluid. Galaxy published not one but two opinion polls, the first giving Labor the generally accepted lead of 52–48, and the second saying it was line ball. But then the bible, Newspoll, said Labor had a ten-point lead. In spite of this, the commentators insisted that a great many Labor seats were at risk and that Tony Abbott was breathing down Julia Gillard's neck, which sounded very much like sexual harassment. Gillard, unfazed, took off around the marginals of Brisbane, Sydney and Melbourne, with a brief detour to Townsville; she promised to extend the education rebate to cover school uniforms and to create trades cadetships and work-experience positions. Abbott stuck to the capitals and promised to extend the education rebate still further to cover almost everything, only to be told that he had grossly underestimated the cost.

Money was always going to be a problem for the Opposition. Campaigning on a platform of ending waste, stopping taxes and paying off debt made it hard to promise anything at all. Abbott attempted to get around this by claiming massive savings could be made, but it turned out a lot of what he was claiming as savings were not savings at all; they came from things like canning the investment in national broadband and selling off Medibank Private. More importantly, there was a contradiction at the heart of the policy: if paying off debt and deficit were really so vital, then why was he promising not to collect $10.5 billion in a Minerals Resource Rent Tax the big miners were quite ready to pay?

But even this was not Abbott's biggest problem in the first week. One item in the promised savings was to make the trade unions pay the Electoral Commission the cost of conducting secret ballots for them. This was a throwback to WorkChoices – in fact, it was worse; even the Howard government had paid 20 per cent of the cost. And it was in direct contradiction of the *Fair Work Act* which Abbott, under enormous pressure, had promised faithfully to leave untouched. Opposition legal advice – well, George Brandis – claimed that a change could be made to the *Electoral Act* to override the offending clause, but even if it worked this would surely be seen as mean and tricky, an underhand attempt to sneak bits of WorkChoices back into legislation. Abbott spent days trying to make people believe he had really killed off the policy, but no one would believe him. Eventually he gave in, and vowed that not only was WorkChoices dead, buried and cremated (though not necessarily in that order), but that no aspect of the *Fair Work Act* would be touched – not now, not for three years, not ever.

The promise was greeted with stunned incredulity. For months, Abbott and his colleagues had been railing against Labor's policy, claiming it obstructed growth and productivity, took industrial relations back to the pre-Keating era, and was a certain recipe for disaster. They had specifically promised amendments, notably to the unfair-dismissal provisions and to the abolition of workplace agreements. Now these solemn undertakings to the Liberal Party's core constituency, small business, were to be abandoned for electoral expediency. It was a huge blow to Abbott's credibility, potentially as damaging to him as the postponement of an emissions trading scheme had been to the former prime minister.

Industrial reform had always been a core – even the core – Liberal belief. From Alfred Deakin through Robert Menzies, Malcolm Fraser and John Howard, it had been the defining policy. Abbott himself, as Howard's minister for employment and workplace relations, was an enthusiastic part of the process, and while he had expressed doubts about the political wisdom of introducing WorkChoices, he had never resiled from much of the substance: 'It was good for wages, it was good for jobs and it was good for workers, never forget that,' he had proclaimed just a few weeks earlier. But it was to be forgotten now.

The Liberals' leader, it appeared, believed in nothing, had no real convictions or principles; he was utterly poll-driven, incapable of making hard decisions or even following a coherent political path. Rather than attempting to defend his own platform, he would betray and sell out his most loyal supporters. It was a hell of an end to a pretty bad first week, redeemed only by a brief appearance on *Hey Hey It's Saturday*, during which he was interviewed by a puppet duck named Plucka.

Gillard meanwhile had her own problems, the chief of which was population policy. Having followed Tony Abbott in rejecting Rudd's affirmation of a Big Australia, she was now urged to say what she would do about it. Well, she said, she had asked her minister, Tony Burke, for a review. She also thought more could be done to get the crowds out of the cities and suburbs and into the regions where they were really needed. But how? Well, there was a review. True; and it would no doubt discover that successive governments had been trying to achieve the same aim since 1970, with no discernible effect. Then Gillard insisted that the population debate was not about immigration. It wasn't? Then what was it about, stopping Australians copulating? Let's change the subject.

The good news was that Labor and the Greens had agreed to a preference deal which would give the Greens a big leg-up in the Senate, where they could realistically hope to hold the balance of power, and could save a significant number of Labor marginals in the House of Representatives. But that was about the only good news; the campaign seemed destined to be even duller, flatter and more micro-managed than its lamentable predecessors. Any attempt at spontaneity or levity was to be ruthlessly suppressed. Joe Hockey made a mildly risqué reference to Paris Hilton and was jumped on by the thought police. Peter Costello essayed a harmless send-up of Julia Gillard's accent and was upbraided for his lack of gallantry. A Labor staffer dressed in red budgie smugglers confronted Tony Abbott and was assailed with demands for his dismissal. And this was only in the first week – four to go. How could we hope to avoid going catatonic with boredom?

Certainly not by tuning in to Julia Gillard's climate change policy. As expected, there was more money for renewable energy and more money to connect it to the grid. There was a promise that no more really dirty power stations would be built, bribes to get old cars off the roads and to make commercial buildings more eco-friendly. Worthy and predictable, but still a non-policy: as Gillard herself had pointed out over and over again, you can't be serious about climate change without putting a price on carbon, and that remained off the agenda until at least 2012. And just to prove she wasn't even remotely serious, she announced that she would appoint a citizens' assembly, which, under the guidance of a commission of experts, would be expected to provide public consensus on the subject. Where they led, she would follow – well, probably, and in due course. Even in a campaign distinguished by cop-outs, this was gold-medal stuff – easily the silliest and most pusillanimous proposal to date. And no one took it seriously.

For starters, there were a few problems. Would the assembly (and for that matter the commission) include the self-interested and sceptical? It would be unrepresentative if it didn't and unworkable if it did. And in any case, we already had a citizen's assembly called parliament, as had been pointed out by numerous critics, Tony Abbott among them. At least he had produced his own non-policy on climate change all by himself. But after his less-than-Churchillian performance on industrial relations, he was hardly in a position to accuse Gillard of political cowardice. Pots and kettles, glass houses etc. Of course, the voters were the real losers. Never had the prime ministership of Australia been contested by such a pair of abject, craven, weak-kneed, whey-faced, chicken-hearted, lily-livered, jelly-bellied milksops. And what a lead-up to the so-called Great Debate: The Wimp versus The Wuss.

The debate had been rescheduled so as not to clash with a

popular cooking program, but it is likely that the only ones who paid it any real attention were the audiences paid to do so by the television networks, and political tragics who had already taken sides. The latter barracked for their own corner and awarded points accordingly, while the former gave the prize to Julia Gillard. Or at least the women did; the men were more evenly split, and if they had any preference at all, it appeared to be for Tony Abbott. The width of the gender gap was about the only thing the exercise contributed to the sum of human knowledge; the rest of it was so bland as to suggest that the hour should have been sponsored by Mogadon.

Both leaders followed their well-prepared scripts, avoided any gaffes, were unfailingly polite and totally unconvincing. It was like a strictly formalised school debate in which the teams are given a topic and told to prepare a case for one side or the other. They then receive points for matter, manner and method – but not for aggression, passion or conviction, since they are not expected to believe in anything they are saying. There were a couple of bright spots: Gillard was enthusiastic on education and Abbott got in the odd crack about Kevin Rudd. But neither had anything new to say and neither managed to bring new life to the slogans, clichés and platitudes they had been repeating since the start of the campaign and before it.

In the circumstances it was silly to talk about who won and who lost because there was no real contest. The whole thing would be well and truly forgotten by polling day; indeed, it would probably have faded from memory by the time the voters read next morning's headlines. And the debate was supposed to be the high point of the campaign, the crucial battle that could mean the difference between victory and defeat. In the event, or rather the non-event, Gillard probably did slightly better, if only because she was generally positive while Abbott was relentlessly negative; he had obviously given up hope of winning the election in his own right and was relying on the government to lose it. But in a sense he could claim to have finished ahead on the night, simply because he wasn't far behind: prime ministers are expected to beat Opposition leaders clearly, so a near-draw in fact counts as a loss.

And Abbott wanted more debates. At least they would distract attention from his policies. One topic raised in the debate had been population, a subject on which the politicians were more than somewhat sensitive. This was because their calls for what Gillard called a sustainable Australia and Abbott bluntly described as lower immigration were utterly out of tune with most commentators. Gillard had been lambasted in the media, particularly in the *Australian*; Abbott had so far escaped relatively unscathed, which seemed a little odd seeing it was he who had started the argument, but then, we were talking about the *Australian*. And both sides were accusing the other of obfuscation: neither had been prepared to talk about real cutbacks or to put a figure on what they considered desirable. But now Abbott took the plunge, or at least stuck a toe in the water: together with his attack dogs, Scott Morrison and Cory Bernardi, he announced that the Coalition would reduce the immigration intake from 300,000 to 170,000 and peg population increase to 1.4 per cent.

This might have sounded good in the western suburbs but there was a slight difficulty: the figures were arrant nonsense. It was true that immigration had reached 300,000 in 2008–09 as a result of the policies of the Howard government, but when the rorts that allowed overseas students to become permanent residents were fixed, it had started falling rapidly: the figure for 2009–10 was 230,000 and the projection for 2010–11 was

175,000, and for 2011–12, 145,000, fewer than Abbott's promise. What was worse, the projection of a population of 36 million by 2050, which had started the whole argument and which Abbott thought was wildly excessive, was based on a yearly increase of just 1.2 per cent; Abbott's policy would result in more, not less. Then there was the question of who would be cut; Abbott ruled out refugees and skilled migrants, so that left family reunion. But this meant wives, husbands, children: were the skilled migrants expected to leave them behind? It was all too silly to contemplate. Such was the great population debate. The Business Council of Australia dismissed it as populist rhetoric, which was gross flattery.

It was incidents like this that made my passionate 37-year-old daughter swear she was abandoning politics for good: she would vote informal. She could not bring herself to vote for Gillard; but if Malcolm Turnbull had been standing instead of Tony Abbott, she might even have voted Liberal, an aberration hitherto unthinkable. I was, of course, horrified, but I could see her point. I was considering breaking the habit of a lifetime and voting for the Greens in the Senate; most of their policies were silly, but at least they were serious about climate change. And mainstream politics seemed incapable of being serious about anything. We were sorely missing Kevin Rudd; he may have been an unlovable administrator, a paranoid control freak and a lousy communicator, but at least he stood for something, or once had. Perhaps it was this that made his enemies so determined to kill him off politically. A story was leaked to the ABC about him missing meetings of the National Security Committee and even sending his young staffer Alister Jordan in his place. This was obviously damaging, but given that the leak was blatantly malicious, it needed to be treated with some suspicion. Even Gillard came to Rudd's defence. But his return to any position of power and influence in Australia was looking less and less likely. It was known he had been offered a part-time role with the United Nations, and this could probably be parlayed into something bigger. The prophet was not without honour, internationally. The temptation to leave the country, or at least the party, that had rejected him must have been increasing.

Not that he was Robinson Crusoe. Just when you thought the campaign could not become any more trivial, it did. On Tuesday 27 July, a day which will live in journalistic infamy, the *Australian* devoted almost the whole of its principal page of election coverage to a series of stories (so-called) about Julia Gillard's ear lobes, dress sense and live-in lover. Next day Janet Albrechtsen wrote a self-indulgent piece admitting that she had now gone off Julia and was back into Tony. And after toying with announcements about suicide prevention, marine parks and rail links in Queensland, both leaders fell into a swooning embrace with that super-tough girl with lots of attitude and big black boots, Laura Norder. Laura is usually exhumed from the political gutter during state election campaigns; she is, after all, a state responsibility. But Gillard promised to invoke her to safeguard the populace against knives, knuckledusters and gas guns for sharks, while Abbott claimed her as his ally in a crackdown on gangs. In these circumstances, the news that the Family First Party had approached the Australian Sex Party seeking a preference deal seemed entirely credible. Even the sight of Julie Bishop on *The Chaser* program, using her famous death stare to destroy a garden gnome, was par for the course. It was that sort of campaign.

To everyone's relief, Abbott tried to get things back on track. Labor had been having some success getting stuck into his proposal for a 1.7 per cent levy on big business to pay for his parental leave scheme. This would inevitably be passed on to the consumer and raise the cost of living: it was a Coles and Woolworths tax. A good line, even if the effect would have been marginal, but Abbott felt he had to counter it. Labor had promised to reduce all company taxes by 1 per cent; Abbott upped the ante to one and a half. But how was this to be funded? Well, a lot of it would come from the cut already promised by Labor.

But hang on. That cut was funded by Labor's Minerals Resource Rent Tax, which Abbott had promised not to implement. Oh well, he had never been that keen on economics anyway. Then there was his climate change policy; he had promised to meet the target of a 5 per cent reduction in emissions by 2020 without a carbon tax; $3.2 billion had been set aside for the exercise. But Treasury estimated it would cost $27 billion to reach the target by Abbott's means, and it turned out that the cost of converting just one coal-fired power station to natural gas would cost almost all of Abbott's $3.2 billion over the ten years and still leave another thirty-four stations to go.

Under normal circumstances this clear evidence of innumeracy would have been devastating, but these were not normal circumstances because Labor was once again fragmenting: the battle of the leaks was back on. It had started two days before the election was called, with Laurie Oakes's story about Gillard welshing on her promise to postpone moving against Rudd. Then the ABC had its scoop about Rudd snubbing meetings of the National Security Committee, which looked a lot like payback. Now Oakes returned with a story about how Gillard had opposed pension rises and paid parental leave in cabinet, which was confirmed independently by Peter Hartcher in the *Sydney Morning Herald*. Just how long was the tit-for-tat to continue? Gillard replied forcefully that she had not opposed the policies but had simply wanted to make sure they were affordable – a reasonable and even commendable stance. Even her critics agreed that she looked pretty prime ministerial in doing so.

But the real story was the leak itself and the instability it demonstrated. Hartcher claimed to have got the story from 'government members,' which, interpreted strictly, would mean cabinet ministers. Given that most of them presumably wanted to continue in the job after winning the election, this seemed improbable. The exceptions, John Faulkner and Lindsay Tanner, were both seen as sea-green incorruptibles and above suspicion, except by Alan Jones, who strayed perilously close to defaming Tanner. Rudd himself formally denied being the source, although his staff members did not. It looked very messy but, as Wayne Swan pointed out, a witch hunt would be even more so and probably pointless anyway. We would just have to soldier on. Then there was yet another leak, this time to the *Australian*, which claimed that Gillard had been even more contemptuous of National Security Committee meetings than Rudd, at one stage sending a former bodyguard to stand in for her. Things were rapidly rolling out of control. And the good news – low inflation figures and falling unemployment, a double which would normally have guaranteed the government's re-election – went almost unnoticed. So, in the general hubbub, did Tony Abbott, which was obviously good for the Coalition. The less he appeared in public, the more he appeared a credible alternative.

It was at this stage that I first realised that Labor could actually lose the election. Of course, I'd previously had qualms, but had been convinced that whatever doubts voters might have, the favourable economic situation and the sheer awfulness of the Opposition front bench would be enough to quell any movement for change; there was, after all, no obvious need for it. Labor's campaign had admittedly been abysmally bad, but the Coalition's had been pretty awful too. However, the leaks had provided the catalyst Abbott needed. The talk about waste and incompetence suddenly gripped: if the government was so preoccupied with tearing itself apart, perhaps it really was unfit to continue in office. And just two weeks into the campaign a Fairfax/Nielsen poll confirmed the trend. Labor's primary vote had plummeted to 36 per cent and the Coalition was now in a winning position. And the huge irony was that Labor was now looking to the man it had sacrificed as being a dead-set loser, Kevin Rudd, to save it.

Apparently Rudd had been approached early in the campaign to visit some of the endangered Queensland marginals and had said that he'd think about it. To date he had stuck to his own seat of Griffith and confined himself to local issues; his only sign of protest had been to remove the ALP logo from his campaign material, just as Malcolm Turnbull had excised all mention of the Liberal Party from his campaign in Wentworth. Now, on the eve of being rushed to hospital for an emergency operation to remove his gall bladder, he issued a statement saying yes, he would be willing to serve wherever he was needed. Gillard said she was wishing him a speedy recovery – indeed, praying for it. From an avowed atheist, this was indeed a sign of desperation.

The former room-temperature foreign minister Alexander Downer – not so much desperate as poisonous – waited until Kevin Rudd was safely sedated and then accused him of acting as a conduit for Downer's own malicious, disloyal and possibly illegal leaks. When Rudd regained consciousness and threatened to sue, Downer claimed to have been misunderstood – it made a change from his usual refrain of 'I cannot recall.' The *Sunday Telegraph* published a full transcript which proved that not only had Downer not been misunderstood, but that he had been unusually straightforward; he said that while he did not use the word 'cunt,' Rudd was a fucking awful person. And Julie Bishop was still tutting at Rudd for swearing.

Could the campaign get any sillier? You betcha. Labor was running a series of ads using direct quotations from Tony Abbott. Abbott was outraged: this was a monstrous smear campaign. Come again? They were his words – had he been smearing himself? I was reminded of a line used by Gough Whitlam in the 1969 campaign: 'I have an agreement with Mr Gorton. If he doesn't tell lies about me, I won't tell the truth about him.' Obviously Abbott felt that telling the truth about him was frightfully unfair. The truth was, of course, that Abbott had always been a political weathervane, a chameleon adept at telling various audiences what he thought they wanted to hear: consistency irrelevant. It seemed to be working: Newspoll agreed that all the momentum was with the Opposition and that Abbott, with leads in Queensland, New South Wales and Western Australia, was on course for victory.

So Gillard decided that if she couldn't beat him, she might as well join him. She was, she announced, throwing away the rulebook: from now on she would be herself, the real Julia. 'You're going to see a whole lot more of me,' she promised the electorate, invoking the prospect of Australia's first nude campaign. Abbott, one felt, would be in it like a flash, or at least a flasher. It turned out to be a touch less exciting: Gillard and Swan rode on the press bus from Sydney to Newcastle, a democratic gesture whose main effect was to stifle the free and frank exchange of views among the hacks. And the announcements went on: extending Family Tax Benefit A to cover dependent children to the age of eighteen, a low-fee superannuation scheme, more autonomy for school principals. But the main thrust was to try and pull Abbott onto her ground. She accepted an offer from Channel 7 for a second debate, provided it was on the economy. Abbott refused, saying it would clash with his grand opening on the following Sunday. Gillard said anywhere, anytime. Abbott still refused: he had a full schedule of weighty engagements, like filleting fish in supermarkets and kicking footballs at schools. Gillard had said there would only be one debate and when he asked for more, she said no. But perhaps, with the new Gillard, no didn't always mean no ...

This lame attempt at levity was horribly reminiscent of Alexander Downer's joke about his domestic-violence policy being concerned with 'the things that batter,' to go with his slogan 'the things that matter.' It was hardly stretching political correctness to say that domestic violence was not a subject for humour, and nor was rape, for which the phrase 'no means no' was coined. Instead of apologising and getting on with it, Abbott tried to justify, explain and wriggle free. The Liberal apparatchiks grimaced. They had been congratulating themselves on having kept him under control and bland. He had even been commendably on message; no matter how vague, self-contradictory or incoherent the message had been, he had stuck to it. Now, just as the polls showed that the women who had adamantly refused to vote for him for months – for years – for a lifetime – were finally ready to come across, he had shaken his dick at them again. Was the real Tony Abbott, the unelectable one, coming back? Well, not yet. His rejigged parental-leave scheme, the third version in a month, emerged without incident and he went to Queensland to talk about tourism, pursued by Gillard yelling, 'It's the economy, stupid!' Abbott pretended he thought she was talking to somebody else.

He went back to wooing the seniors at a bowls club and was mobbed by blue-rinse lady bowlers who obviously thought Julia was asking for it. Gillard, in response, promised to fast-track the baby bonus. The lady bowlers, unmoved, continued to embrace Abbott.

And meanwhile Kevin Rudd prepared to rise from his hospital bed to defend his record. Rudd had a lot riding on the campaign, which was why the suggestion that he was somehow behind the attempts to sabotage it was so stupid. His loyalty was not in question, and nor was his eagerness to be part of a new Labor government. More than that, his legacy was on the line. Abbott was pledged to reverse his health reforms, abort his education revolution and shelve his national broadband network; and on the broader front, an Abbott victory would ratify the accusations of waste and incompetence that had been the basis of the Opposition campaign. Kevin Rudd would be relegated to a footnote in history, an almost accidental prime minister in the mould of John Gorton or even Billy McMahon. Rudd indeed had an interest in preventing Abbott from sliding into government by default, and his commitment to preventing this happening was absolute.

As the campaign passed its halfway point, the prospect looked more likely than not, although a change of government in the prevailing circumstances would clearly be a breach of political tradition, indeed almost of natural law. Australia, having been the only advanced country to avoid recession, was now experiencing the economic double of falling unemployment and falling inflation. Interest rates were a lot lower than they had been when the government came to office and were unlikely to rise beyond what was seen as normal levels. Australia had the lowest debt in the industrialised world and the budget was forecast to return to surplus within three years.

The mining boom had meant that some parts of the country were doing better than others, but everyone was doing pretty well and both business and consumer confidence ratings were high. Seen from the point of view of the hip pocket, things could hardly have been rosier. And yet the voters were preparing to vote the government that had presided over this happy state and was at least partly responsible for it out of office after one truncated term. Instead, they planned to install a mob of shop-soiled has-beens and wild-eyed never-will-bes whose policies consisted of slashing government services, refusing to collect the taxes with which to pay off what they absurdly insisted was unsustainable debt, and sending asylum seekers to Nauru.

The government had certainly not been perfect, but it had been a lot better than fair: the ministry, with very few exceptions, had been at least competent and frequently excellent – certainly the best first-term executive since Bob Hawke's 1983 all-stars. Tony Abbott's front bench, by contrast, was the worst in living memory. Andrew Robb and Greg Hunt were both worth their places; Ian Macfarlane, George Brandis and Peter Dutton were honest toilers. With a bit more experience Julie Bishop, Joe Hockey and Christopher Pyne would be adequate in junior portfolios. But that was about it. There were senior shadows who were never seen and seldom heard of: how many voters could have named Abbott's spokesman on defence? (David Johnston. See, I told you.) Most of the rest might as well not have been there at all. In government they would be frankly embarrassing and in some cases dangerous – ambitious opportunists like Scott Morrison and fanatics like Sophie Mirabella were a sure recipe for instability. And the residue of the Howard years, Kevin Andrews, Bronwyn Bishop and Philip Ruddock, were best forgotten.

But given that they might well be back on the Treasury benches in a little over a fortnight, there was no time for comfortable amnesia. The best Labor could hope for now was that the malaise in New South Wales and especially in Queensland could be contained. On the last poll figures, Labor could lose sixteen seats in those two states alone, with only a small hope of making gains in its strongholds of Victoria, South Australia and the ACT. This left Western Australia, where things were never good, Tasmania, always a lottery, and the Northern Territory, where one Labor seat was a knife-edge proposition. The only good news for Labor's faithful was that most people still expected them to win, which in the past had been a good sign, and that the bookies had them as firm favourites, and the bookies had never been wrong – so far. But given that almost everything about the 2010 election was setting one or another precedent, it was not that much comfort.

> *'I think the puppet on the right shares my beliefs.'*
> *'I think the puppet on the left is more to my liking.'*
> *'Hey, wait a minute, there's one guy holding out*
> *both puppets!'*—BILL HICKS

★ 13.

THE REALLY GOOD NEWS was that, to the surprise of nearly everyone and the delight of most, the High Court upheld an appeal run by the GetUp! organisation and overturned the iniquitous legislation of the Howard government which cut short the time new voters could enrol once an election was called. It appeared that the law was not only undemocratic but unconstitutional. The full ramifications of the decision would not be known until the court published its detailed judgment, but the immediate result was that about 100,000 people who had been deprived of their right to vote could now turn up at the polling booths. This was a huge win, not just for the new voters but for the whole country and indeed for democracy itself. Let's hear it for GetUp!

And a few days later the polls showed a slight swing back to Labor; not enough to really matter, but it suggested that the government was no longer in free fall. This figured; there was a lot of grumbling but no signs of a real movement for change. That was the good news, and not just for Labor: the electorate retained some residue of commonsense. But the situation remained highly volatile; the numbers varied wildly across the country, not just from state to state but from electorate to electorate. In the national polls, New South Wales and Queensland showed up as disaster areas for Labor, with Western Australia not much better, but local surveys suggested that the government could well hold on to Eden-Monaro, Leichhardt and Hasluck, all of which should have been pushovers for the Coalition. They still might be; there was plenty of time for the kind of unexpected development that would produce a decisive swing one way or the other, and if the awful campaign had one thing going for it, it was the capacity to produce the unexpected.

Labor, of course, was hoping it would come from Tony Abbott, but his minders appeared to have him firmly back under control. All his public events, up to and including his gala (or perhaps galah) launch were now so contained as to be positively sterile – so much for real action, a concept which was always as bizarre as real Julia. Unless Abbott could be goaded into the open by taunts of cowardice, Labor would have to rely on its own devices, which now consisted mainly of hopes and prayers that the Kevin Rudd intervention did not run out of control and blow the whole campaign to smithereens. They had some success: the Liberal Party guardians were persuaded that Abbott had to break cover, so after weeks of procrastination he agreed to appear on the *7.30 Report* on the day of the unveiling of the Liberals' alternative to Labor's national broadband network. He had not actually attended the unveiling himself, which was probably just as well; on the *7.30 Report* he confessed that he was not a tech-head and hadn't a clue what it was all about, which was, in any case, not very much.

Gillard, meanwhile, went back to her home ground on education to announce financial rewards for good schools and good teachers, which was just what the conservatives wanted to hear and the progressives didn't – like most of her education reforms, it was pitched firmly at the right. Still, it was less alarming than a previous promise to provide 1000 new chaplains for schools – what was she thinking? Perhaps it was the tropical atmosphere of Darwin, where the announcement was made; a couple of days later, Julie Bishop succumbed to the climate and was photographed patting a cane toad. Why was it, she murmured, that everyone else got to kiss babies and she got the toads? No one was tactless enough to respond. A less diplomatic role was taken by Andrew Peacock, who, while campaigning in his old safe seat of Kooyong, mused that, 'You'd need to be pretty handicapped not to appreciate that this government is dissolving before your eyes daily.' The wrath of those representing the disabled was all the greater because Labor's candidate for the seat, the barrister Steve Hurd, was in fact legally blind.

I finally had to admit it: this election campaign was not dull at all. Depressing, maddening, infantile, an insult to the voters' intelligence and a travesty of the democratic process – but not dull. Just look at the cast of characters: supporting, or more often opposing, Julia Gillard and Tony Abbott we had Kevin Rudd, John Howard, Bob Hawke, Paul Keating and Malcolm Fraser – every living prime minister except Gough Whitlam, and surely it was only a matter of time before he issued a crushing edict from his imperial couch. Then there were the pretenders: John Hewson, Peter Costello, Malcolm Turnbull, Andrew Peacock and, most absurdly of all, Mark Latham as a *60 Minutes* journalist with a licence to make a complete dickhead of himself.

A farcical plotline in which heroes and villains are essentially interchangeable and political certainties change scene by scene: nothing is constant or believable. And the dialogue: could the great absurdists Harold Pinter, Eugene Ionesco or

Samuel Beckett ever have produced such a barrage of meaningless waffle? From a policy point of view, the campaign was like a game of soccer in which both teams did little more than pass the ball backwards and forwards between the defenders and the only chance of a score was if a goalie fell over and let in an own goal. But just look at the half-time entertainment: the clowns on the sidelines, and the melodramatic pratfalls and phoney carry-on by the players. No, it wasn't dull, but it was awful beyond parody.

And just when you thought it might be getting somewhere sensible – with Julia Gillard making a firm commitment to buy back as much water as was needed to restore the Murray–Darling Basin and following it with a warm, authoritative and convincing performance on *Q&A* – it all went haywire again as she reached into the pork barrel to produce the biggest pig of all: $2.1 billion for a Sydney suburban rail link which had been promised and discarded for the last fifteen years. Sure, it wasn't a bad idea, but only as part of a long–term, integrated transport plan. In the middle of an election campaign, it was just a big pig, and one that wouldn't even attempt to fly for another four years. More instructive was a debate between the treasurer, Wayne Swan, and his counterpart, Joe Hockey. Swan had some claim to being the world's most successful treasurer; Australia's miracle economy had just been pronounced the envy of all developed countries by Nobel Prize winner Joseph Stiglitz and the latest outlook from the Reserve Bank was unequivocally confident and upbeat. He was effortlessly on top of his subject and took all the points for content. Hockey, though, was adjudged to have had the better style, so the commentators awarded the debate to him. These, remember, were the same commentators who had spent the entire campaign complaining that there was not enough substance and too much spin. A letter-writer to the

Sydney Morning Herald, Allan Walker, put it neatly: 'The difference between the parties is that Labor is incapable of selling success and the Liberals are very capable of selling fear.'

Tony Abbott proceeded to prove as much at his launch, which contained no new policies at all: he described the government as 'the worst in Australia's history' (Brisbane lord mayor Campbell Newman, even more prone to hyperbole, had called it 'a socialist dictatorship') and spent a large part of his speech on boat people. He had already spoken to the president of Nauru (but shouldn't that have been the prime minister? Oh no, that was East Timor, where they actually have a government) and his spokesman, Scott Morrison (the new Philip Ruddock), had visited the island and found that they were ready, willing and eager to reopen the detention hell-hole (which he later described as being 'a bit like boarding school' – I doubt if his *alma mater*, Riverview College, would appreciate the comparison) if the price was right. The launch concluded with a lengthy embrace from John Howard, perhaps not the ideal image for what was supposed to be a new, vibrant, grown-up government. Malcolm Fraser, asked if Abbott was ready for government, replied simply: 'No.'

Julia Gillard was having her own troubles with a former leader. Mark Latham had been cynically employed by Channel Nine to invade political meetings under the pretence of making a television special – well, actually, someone competent would make the special and he would do a bit of ranting. The move was greeted with horror and contempt, especially by Nine's incomparable political editor Laurie Oakes (after all, up to now he had been one of the stars of the campaign), but Latham and the channel pressed ahead. Network supremo David Gyngell did apologise for Latham's behaviour in confronting Gillard but did nothing to rein him in. Another day, another distraction.

And of course the rest of the media were all terribly censorious and filmed and spoke and wrote about nothing else. This meant that Latham's abortive encounters with Abbott and Gillard had one beneficial side-effect: the spotlight was off Kevin Rudd, whose successful evasion of Latham also meant that he became invisible to the media as a whole. But otherwise his whistle-stop tour of the Queensland marginals seemed ineffective; if anything the swing against Labor in the Sunshine State firmed up. And New South Wales was not looking much better.

Things came to a head in what was billed as a town hall-style public forum in the RSL club in the suburb of Rooty Hill, forty-two kilometres west of Sydney's CBD (and no, it was named because of the roots of trees, not the other kind). The venue was conveniently centred on the electorates of Lindsay, Macquarie and Greenway (marginal Labor) and Hughes (marginal Liberal) and is also believed to have a psychological and psephological affinity with other Labor marginals such as Robertson and Dobell on the New South Wales mid-north coast. Assuming even a small proportion of these voters were watching or listening, Gillard and Abbott had a lot to win or lose on their performances. Fortunately for Gillard and Labor, not a lot *were* able to watch or listen, because the event was the exclusive property of the Sydney *Daily Telegraph* and Sky News, which refused to make a feed available to the free-to-air networks. Thus the full performance was seen by just half the number who watched the political satire of *The Gruen Transfer* and *Yes We Canberra* on the ABC.

From the start the prime minister was in trouble; she was first up and positioned on stage on a barstool, which made her look a little like a witch impaled on a stake. The questions were pretty hostile, and although she handled them clearly and competently, she always looked out of her natural habitat.

Abbott, by contrast, was greeted as a soul mate, came down to the audience's level and was rewarded with a series of Dorothy Dixers. The surprise was that the punters at the club only gave him a narrow win; according to the *Daily Telegraph* readers' poll, he romped it in, although that probably says as much about the *Tele* as it does about the event. Understandably buoyed, Abbott said he thought it was a great forum and there should be more of them and everyone should be allowed to watch – indeed, they should be compelled. But he continued to duck Gillard's challenge to an actual debate.

The two resumed their barnstorming of marginal seats and the rain of pork continued unabated, but some actual policies appeared: Abbott announced free pharmaceuticals for veterans and said he would build a lot of technical colleges, presumably to replace the trade training centres the government was already constructing. This seemed unnecessary and wasteful and once more drew attention to the cost of the promises, which, after an austere start, now seemed to have got back to the normal campaign level. Both sides had insisted there would be no new net expenditures; all their commitments would be offset by savings, and all their accounting would be submitted to Treasury under the Howard government's much-trumpeted charter of budget honesty.

There were, of course, a few fudges: both sides announced plans which would not involve real money for four years or so, and therefore did not need to be costed for the forthcoming term. The government also used money which had been quietly set aside in its May budget to pay for new projects. But there was a general pretence of financial rectitude, although each side made ritual claims of the other's chicanery. The government, led ably by financial services minister Chris Bowen, had more success: he was able to point to instances of double counting and simple error in Opposition documents, and Abbott was forced to admit that there might have been 'a few typos' – several hundred million dollars' worth, actually. But the crunch came when the *Sydney Morning Herald* published a Treasury document pointing out that the Opposition had underestimated the cost of one promise by $800 million. Abbott cried foul; this was a deliberate leak, and showed that the government could not be trusted. What it showed was that the Coalition couldn't add up; and there was no reason for such information to be confidential. But Abbott used the revelation as an excuse to say the Opposition would cost its own promises in future and would employ a private accountant to verify its figures. And the heck with the charter of budget honesty. Under other circumstances this might have been a serious matter, but the public was by now so jaded and cynical about election promises that it passed almost unnoticed.

It was something of a relief when Gillard announced a real policy on climate change – well, as real as a policy which did not put a price on carbon could be. It attempted to control the level of carbon emissions by allowing farmers to verify and receive credits for any measures they took to reduce emissions and then trade the credits for real money on the international market. In Abbott's version the government would pick the winners and the Australian taxpayers would foot the bill; in Gillard's it would be run independently and paid for by international polluters. It was a vast improvement, a policy worth spruiking, and she conveniently chose to spruik it at the Wollongbar Agricultural Institute in my neighbouring electorate of Page, so I went along to watch. The prime minister was late, but the hacks who were following her on the campaign trail were used to that. It had not, one veteran confessed, been a jolly four weeks – not nearly as much fun as it had been with Kevin Rudd three years earlier. But the mood on the bus was reasonably upbeat. More so, it turned out, among the camera crews than the journos; more than ever, the campaign was all about television events.

Thus Gillard together with Penny Wong and Tony Burke – a ministerial triptych – were delivered to a paddock whose rural tranquillity was disturbed only by the roar of traffic on the adjacent highway and a barking dog, presumably of National Party tendencies. A group of cows was mustered for the occasion; the prime minister, resplendent in jeans and cowboy boots, resisted the temptation to inquire if they were mooooving forward. She chatted to the farm workers, had a cup of tea and ate quite a lot of blueberries supplied by a local admirer. Finally, after all traces of bullshit had been removed from camera range, she made the big announcement and settled down to the usual questions from a youngish press pack – the heavies had by now bailed out to pontificate. The hacks were a lot more friendly than I remembered them being with Rudd, and it was all pretty low-key. The prime minister was content to be simply Julia, real or not. She appeared in good spirits, cool and controlled, and there was never any risk that she would lose the script. But somehow it was a bit of a letdown; I had been hoping for more passion leading into the final week.

Perhaps she was saving it for when and where it was really needed; although Page is notionally marginal and would be swallowed if the predicted state swing to the Coalition was consistent, the local member, Janelle Saffin, has been hard-working and popular and has delivered plenty of goodies. My bet was that she would hang on. But this wasn't what the pollsters were saying: the weekend polls varied between a narrow Labor win and a narrow Labor loss, with a hung parliament now a very real possibility. What everyone agreed was that Labor would lose a swag of seats in New South Wales and Queensland – as many as seventeen and still counting. And that was the ball game, before Western Australia and the Northern Territory even started counting. There could be a couple of gains in Victoria and South Australia, and Tasmania, as always, was unpredictable. Once again it was an exciting election – not because of the vision, skill and unpredictability of the players, but simply because it was close.

Ironically, what could have been the big, defining issue emerged only at the death, when it was too late to make enough waves to disturb the now terminally stagnant morass of parochial promises, tit-for-tat squabbles and mindless trivia that the campaign had become. National broadband had been one of the big planks of Kevin Rudd's ambitious platform in 2007, but it had never received as much attention as it deserved because there were other more immediately dramatic contenders for the spotlight, climate change and WorkChoices being the most obvious. But the broadband network was important not just because of its scale but because of its universality: it had implications not only for business but for almost all aspects of life.

Rudd had talked up its central role in his education revolution, and now Julia Gillard belatedly linked it to health: in an otherwise lacklustre launch held just five days before the poll, she linked broadband to health policy, especially as it applied to the rural and regional areas. She promised to make the network available free for patients to hold teleconferences with specialists, saving the need for lengthy and costly travel for follow-up appointments, and also for emergency after-hours calls for parents who needed urgent advice on a sick child. Broadband would quite literally transform the lives of those outside the major cities; and as the commentators belatedly noted, it would also make living and working in the country far more practical and attractive. Broadband was an important part of the solution to the overcrowding in cities, which had provoked the largely misdirected debate on immigration and, by extension, boat people.

The implications were huge, and this was one issue where there was a real and unbridgeable gap between the parties. Labor's proposal was for a near-universal state-of-the-art system to be installed by government – and indeed, the process was already well under way. The Coalition's response was to spend as little as possible and trust the private sector to cobble together some Heath Robinson arrangement, which would be delivered where and when it could be seen to be profitable and would be hopelessly second-rate anyway. It should have been a big winner, a game-breaker, and even at this late stage it seriously wedged the Coalition; clearly the unprofitable regional and remote areas would be the big losers from Tony Abbott's promise to abandon the government program, and the National Farmers' Federation had already pronounced itself in favour of the government policy. The Nationals' leader Warren Truss loyally tried to justify the Coalition – Liberal Party – position, but his heart was not in it. And most of his colleagues preferred to change the subject as quickly as possible. It was perhaps fortunate that, like Abbott himself, they could take refuge in the defence that it was all terribly technical, indeed incomprehensibly so, and they really couldn't be expected to answer questions about it. Had Labor pursued the issue earlier, that excuse would not have worked.

But then, the people running the Labor campaign weren't all that savvy either. The national secretary, Karl Bitar, proved the point when he demanded a 'fulsome' debate on the economy; the last person to misuse the word so spectacularly was John Howard, who used to describe his welcome from George W. Bush as fulsome – although, come to think of it, maybe Howard was being entirely accurate. The to-ing and fro-ing over a debate became a theme for what should have been a vital seventy-two hours as the campaign drew towards what the tabloids laughingly described as its climax. Gillard wanted an hour, face to face; Abbott wanted nothing but was goaded into offering half an hour, which on inspection appeared to consist of consecutive fifteen-minute interviews. Instead he challenged Gillard to another Rooty Hill-style forum, this time in Queensland and on free-to-air television. A flurry of increasingly acerbic letters between the party bosses failed to resolve the impasse and finally Gillard took the same course as she had in her negotiations with the miners: she capitulated. So there was no debate, which meant that Abbott had won the debate and the forum would go ahead on his terms.

In a fit of triumphalism, he claimed that Labor had made Australia a greater investment risk than Botswana and the Congo, and announced a refinement to his asylum-seeker policy: if the navy encountered a boatload of the bastards, the captain would ring him and he himself would make the decision as to whether they were to be turned back. Or perhaps rammed. Or maybe boarded and looted … After medication he agreed that he would, of course, take the captain's advice first. But the final decision would remain with Master and Commander Abbott. It wasn't quite the brain snap that Labor was hoping for, but it showed promise. Unfortunately he was back under control by the time he made his ritual final appearance at the National Press Club, where he launched what he called an 'Economic Action Plan.' Not Real Action? Well, no; the main points were a proposal to pay young people welfare to get off welfare, and to raise money through infrastructure bonds. It would be far cheaper just to borrow the money, but that would be Debt. This was just Waste. Still, the appearance was a success in that he did not say anything really outrageous or fall off the stage. And in keeping with the tedium of the times, both leaders stayed strictly on message in their final interviews with an acerbic and frustrated Kerry O'Brien; even the redoubtable Kezza could not locate an unsedated nerve.

Then it was back to the rain of pork in the marginals and the tornado of attack ads on television and the interminable argument about costing the promises. The Coalition, as anticipated, had sent its list to a private firm whose name it would not reveal; since no one expected the pledges would receive anything other than a tick and perhaps an elephant stamp, this was no longer an issue. Labor had sent its program – most of it – to Treasury. This was also expected to be a formality. Each side continued to snipe at the other, but there was little hope that a major error would appear, or that the public would care all that much if it did; all most people wanted was to get the whole bloody charade over with so they could get back to the important stuff, like footy.

In the circumstances they were remarkably patient and forbearing when an allegedly representative sample was dragooned into the Broncos Leagues Club in Brisbane during the final week for another community forum. Surprisingly, given what the polls had been saying about Queensland, the crowd was much more sensible and civilised than the mob at Rooty Hill, and an authoritative performance by Gillard gave the prime minister a narrow win over the matier but less substantial Abbott. Perhaps the north was not looming as quite the disaster for Labor that had been predicted; this chimed with my own sources, who were now saying that losses could be limited to four or five seats. On the other hand, the bottom seemed to have dropped out of New South Wales; the carnage was now estimated as at least seven and still counting.

And the report of the Coalition's costings finally emerged: to no one's surprise the bean counters at WHK Horwath found that the figures supplied by Joe Hockey and Andrew Robb added up; there were no obvious arithmetical errors and the results were just peachy. Of course, the figures were based on some very hairy assumptions, but those had nothing to do with WHK Horwath. As they say in the trade, garbage in, garbage out. The report caused the odd ripple in the final week, but for all practical purposes the campaign was already over. The final event was Gillard's appearance at the National Press Club; she appeared a little tired, but was still relentlessly on message, totally in control. And for almost the first time since becoming prime minister she allowed herself to relax a little; the authority she was exuding seemed a little less forced than usual, nearly natural. It could almost be said that she sounded prime ministerial. Just as well, responded the pessimists (and there were a lot of them) in the Labor camp. It could be her last chance.

The crowds dispersed, Gillard went on a last sweep through the marginals, and Abbott embarked on a last stunt: he promised to campaign by exhaustion, to stay awake for at least the next thirty-six hours, talking to anyone he could find. Well, he might stay awake, but would his audience? Considering that he had spent most of the campaign trying to prove that he had the gravitas appropriate for Australia's head of government, it seemed an odd way to finish and it gave Gillard the opening for her best crack: 'If you want someone to run a marathon, choose Tony Abbott. If you want someone to run the country, choose me.' But Abbott had the perfect riposte: just look at the polls. Six months ago he was considered unelectable. Now he was so close to the Lodge he could smell it.

> **"** *I've been a puppet, a pauper, a pirate, a poet, a pawn and a king.*—FRANK SINATRA

★ 14.

THE DAY OF RECKONING dawned bright and sunny, but that was the only good thing you could say about it. Saturday 21 August was, by any measure, an inauspicious date – the forty-second anniversary of the day the Russian tanks rolled into Prague, crushing a brief period of hope and democracy. In Australia the prospect was not quite as dire, but it wasn't all that cheerful either.

Determinedly optimistic, the front bar of the Billinudgel Hotel predicted Labor by a whisker. But according to the bookies there had been a surge of late betting on the Coalition: Sportsbet had brought them in to $2.45. Labor was still favourite at $1.53, but that was only because of some very big early bets on the government. Centrebet had Labor slightly shorter at $1.48 as a result of one plunge of $60,000. The Coalition looked like good value at $2.60 and that was where the money was going. Punters have always claimed that the market is a more reliable guide than the polls, but this time it was not giving a clear direction. The betting on the marginals was also all over the place: Labor was considered surprisingly safe in some, but in Bennelong, Liberal John Alexander was an unbackable favourite to defeat Maxine McKew, the Labor heroine who had knocked off John Howard in 2007.

The other heavies, the media, weren't much better. A week earlier, the Sunday blats had broken Labor's way five to one, with the bulk of Rupert Murdoch's evil empire judging that Julia Gillard deserved a second term to prove herself. Now the tide had turned. Led by the *Australian*, the pack overwhelmingly leaned towards Abbott. The exceptions were the *Herald-Sun* and the *Adelaide Advertiser*, but then the swing in Victoria and South Australia was towards Labor, and Rupert had always preferred to be on the winning side. In Sydney, Granny *Herald* stuck with Gillard, but she would, wouldn't she? The majority, namely News Limited, rules. This did not mean that they were enthusiastic about Tony Abbott: quite the reverse. But he was regarded by the custodians of news and views as the least worst alternative.

Abbott himself ended the campaign ranting about the sins, real and imagined, of the government; at least he could claim consistency. But, incredibly, Gillard spent the last twenty-four hours chasing him down the same road of negativity. She sounded not just desperate and panic-stricken, but a trifle unhinged. It was all about Abbott, she raved. He was the great destroyer, the enemy of all that was good and decent. Not only that, he would bring back WorkChoices ... hang on a minute. Gillard was the incumbent, the prime minister. It was her job to be positive about her government: she should have been saying Vote For Me, not Vote Against Him. This was elementary. Either she had acquired a political death wish, or she was still listening to the strategists of Sussex Street, which amounted to the same thing.

Up to this point I had retained a shred of optimism; I had relied on the hope that Labor's expertise in holding its marginal seats against the odds might push the government over the line. It now seemed improbable; any remaining swinging voters would surely have succumbed to Gillard's own despair. It became a matter of what-ifs. What if Gillard had resisted the pressure to make a cynical promise to build the Parramatta to Epping railway, thus aligning and identifying herself with the loathed and doomed regime in Macquarie Street? What if she had rejected the advice to go early and had waited until October to establish herself in the job and take full advantage of the high ground of incumbency? What if she had not accepted the right's blandishments, stayed loyal to Kevin Rudd and been content to wait until after the election when, win, lose or draw, she could have obtained the leadership without the stigma of treachery? What if she had joined Rudd to insist that climate change was indeed the great challenge and the emissions trading scheme should stay front and centre on the government's platform? And, the biggest what-if of all: what if the government had defied the cowardice of the numbers men and gone to a double dissolution on the issue of climate change back in February – just six months earlier?

I spent much of the day in such pointless contemplation, and I wondered if Gillard had the same thoughts as she made her way back to Altona to join the sullen and disgruntled voters, queuing to vote in an election they would rather not have had, to contemplate a choice they did not want to make.

There is a superstition among many political commentators that the nation has a sort of collective mind; that when the voters go to the polls there is a psychic bond between them which determines the overall result. This strange belief manifests itself in newspaper headlines like 'Australia Decides,' as if the entire country had become a single entity for the purpose of determining who should govern it. It is, of course, nonsense:

Australia doesn't decide, individual Australians do. And a close election cannot be taken as evidence that they are in any way ambivalent about their preferences: voter A does not communicate telepathically with voter B to agree, 'If you vote Labor, I'll vote Liberal to balance it out.'

Having said that, there is little doubt that on 21 August a lot of people cast their ballots without a great deal of conviction. I overheard one woman tell a friend that she had changed her mind a hundred times about how to vote, the last time as she was numbering the squares. And there was a larger than usual informal vote – more than 5.5 per cent. It was not clear how much of this was due to Mark Latham's anarchic and irresponsible advice to voters to hand in blank forms, but it certainly suggested a lack of enthusiasm. Politicians tell us that in the end the people always get it right and that their judgment must be respected; but when that judgment is that a large proportion of voters – perhaps even a majority – doesn't really want either of the contenders, it takes a lot of the gloss off the victory.

So in some ways it was almost a relief that, on the night itself, there wasn't a victory to claim. But shortly after we turned on the television and got stuck into the serious drinking, it appeared that there would be: the bloodbath Labor had been fearing in Queensland swiftly became reality and by eight o'clock Labor had lost nine seats in that state alone. Given my calculation that seven was the most Labor could afford, I was ready to concede right there. But then Victoria delivered two seats back, and New South Wales fragmented. The swing picked up five quick seats, but Labor hung on to Dobell, Eden-Monaro, Page and, incredibly, Robertson, all of which should have been swept away by the swing. Even Lindsay, the totemic western suburbs of Sydney seat around which so much of the campaign had centred, remained on a knife-edge. But South

Australia did not come good as Labor had hoped, and Solomon, in the Northern Territory, fell.

We opened another bottle and waited for the west, which turned out to be indecisive: Labor lost its obvious two, which gave the Coalition a net gain of just twelve – well short of the seventeen it needed for a clean win. Labor had also lost Melbourne to the Greens, as widely predicted, and was in imminent danger of losing Denison in Tasmania to the previously Green independent, Andrew Wilkie. But the Coalition, in addition to its two Victorian losses, had mislaid O'Connor in Western Australia to a National, who announced that he would sit on the crossbenches as an independent. Assuming that Labor won the remaining undecided seats, which looked more likely than not since its members were the incumbents in all three and should therefore have the edge in the pre-poll and postal votes still to be counted, this would make the result seventy-two all, with six crossbenchers. Give Labor Adam Bandt, the Melbourne Green, and the Coalition Tony Crook, the O'Connor National, and it was seventy-three all, with four swinging. But the Coalition had decisively outpolled Labor in the primary votes and so could be adjudged the front-runner. This was certainly the way Tony Abbott saw it; having warned his followers against what he termed 'premature triumphalism,' he led them in an orgy of gloating. They cheered and chiacked and booed the name of Julia Gillard, ugly Australians at their worst. I finished the bottle and went to bed to face the ultimate nightmare: a minority Abbott government operating at the whim of Bob Katter.

Fortunately Sunday morning brought more clarity. It had been too easy to assume that the three rural independents – Bob Katter, Tony Windsor and Rob Oakeshott – would side automatically with the Coalition. Certainly they were all former

Nationals and they all represented predominantly conservative electorates; but as the South Australian premier, Mike Rann, who was experienced in such matters, pointed out, they had left the National Party for a reason, and in some cases that reason had opened a bitter rift. Katter spoke of being insulted by the Nationals' leader, Warren Truss, and even by the Senate leader, Barnaby Joyce. Windsor described Joyce as a fool. And all three of them were on record as being solid supporters of Labor's national broadband proposals.

So perhaps, just perhaps, Gillard was in with a chance at minority government; Labor had in fact narrowly won the two-party-preferred vote, for what that was worth. And certainly she would be more comfortable with the incoming Senate than would Abbott. The egregious Steve Fielding was gone, but, incredibly, he had been replaced by a relic from the antediluvian Democratic Labor Party, who owed his election to the Australian Sex Party – another of those little anomalies the Senate system throws up, and we mean throws up. However, the Greens had realised their best hopes and now held at least eight and probably nine Senate seats, which gave them the balance of power. And Bob Brown made it clear they intended to use it. Either major party would find this prospect uncomfortable, but Labor, already in reluctant coalition with the Greens in Tasmania, would probably be less frustrated.

But this was all speculation and fantasy; it would be at least another week before the fat lady was even ready to clear her throat. On the morning after the night before, only one thing was certain: Labor had lost the confidence of most Australians in the space of less than a year, and the architects of the policies, strategies and brain-snaps who had brought this about through their cynicism, cowardice and self-importance should be strung up by their testicles and lashed savagely with bulls' pizzles.

This was a view shared by a great many members of the party itself, although most of them were rather more circumspect in articulating it. The independents were making 'stable government' a priority even before they began serious negotiations. To re-open the blame game with a major shit-fight would be counterproductive, so the tossing of turds was reasonably controlled.

The Queensland premier, Anna Bligh, said it was all the fault of the New South Wales machine men for running to the polls so soon after sacking Kevin Rudd. The national campaign director, Karl Bitar, replied that the biggest losses were in her state and if Queenslanders did not understand the finer distinctions of the federal system it was her fault for not educating them. Two failed candidates, Maxine McKew in New South Wales and Alannah MacTiernan in Western Australia, put the blame squarely on Bitar, and a number of prominent Labor figures including the former Queensland premier Peter Beattie demanded that he be sacked. Julia Gillard hastily ordered Bitar's close friend and colleague Mark Arbib to withdraw from the ABC's *Q&A* in case the show was interrupted by a lynch mob. Fortunately for Labor there were also recriminations on the other side. The New South Wales Liberal powerbroker David Clarke was accused of losing Sydney's western suburbs – and therefore the election – by stuffing the marginal seats with dud candidates, against the wishes of Tony Abbott. Both major parties turned on themselves, which at least meant a pause in hostilities towards each other.

And during this pause the three magi from the bush followed their star to Canberra, there to select the rightful ruler. They were, at the very least, an interesting mob. The most prominent, Tony Windsor from New England, was generally regarded as a man of integrity. He immediately made it clear that he would not be bribed by the promise of a ministry and he was not interested in becoming speaker; he wanted his vote to be free and effective. Stable government was his top priority, but he was specifically concerned about health, water, communications and climate change – big issues which had received little if any attention during the campaign. What he did not mention were his personal obsessions: ending gun control and re-introducing the death penalty, a platform which put him well to the right of Tony Abbott and almost anyone else in the current parliament. He had a lot of tickets on himself and did not suffer fools gladly, particularly when the fool was Barnaby Joyce. He said he would talk to both sides, but if he could not get satisfaction from either, then tough: back to the polls.

Rob Oakeshott from Lyne, centred on Port Macquarie, was a relative newcomer, probably the most idealistic and visionary of the trio, and he had the most ambitious and impractical idea: a relaxation of party lines to form a government with the support of a clear majority of parliament using the best talent from both sides. Both Julia Gillard and Tony Abbott immediately offered to include him in the ministry, but stopped well short of embracing his concept. It was a bit too revolutionary; even during the darkest days of World War II, Australia had not found it necessary to form a government of national unity. Oakeshott shared Windsor's general policy concerns, especially when it came to communications; Abbott quickly made noises about his own proposal for a Mickey Mouse broadband network being pretty flexible, especially when it applied to provincial electorates like Oakeshott's. Interestingly, Oakeshott got on well with Kevin Rudd, as did Rudd's fellow banana-bender Bob Katter, who said publicly that if Rudd had still been leading the Labor Party, he would have found it difficult to withhold his support from his friend.

Katter, from the wilds of Kennedy in outback Queensland, was already well known as one of parliament's resident eccentrics, an outspoken cowboy with a taste for silly hats and his own doggerel. His personal hero was the brilliant but disgraced 'Red Ted' Theodore, the Labor treasurer from the depression years. He had learned his politics from the legendary Country Party leader 'Black Jack' McEwen and his economics from the National Civic Council's Bartholomew Augustine (but just call me Bob) Santamaria. As had Tony Abbott, but Abbott at least claimed to have discarded protectionism; Katter embraced it as the solution to the multiple woes of rural Australia and said he would award the gong to whichever party came up with the commitment (and the money) to save the bush. This of course would include health, water and communications – but not climate change, which he regarded as a citified beat-up. Katter played the loner, the tough guy – he had once threatened to have Liberal Peter Lindsay killed, although he later said that it had merely been a joke, a recantation which disappointed a great many members on both sides of the house. But he insisted he would stay with his fellow musketeers during the course of the negotiations with Gillard and Abbott. After that, all three agreed, it would be every man for himself.

These were the big three; but there were other cross-benchers who may or may not have to be accommodated in the final mix. The Green from Melbourne, Adam Bandt, had always said he would prefer to support Labor, but given the impasse he was willing to talk to the Coalition as well. However, his wish list, which would be very difficult for Labor to fulfil, was seen by the conservatives as right off the planet: first and foremost a carbon price, and then welcoming policies on asylum seekers and gay marriage. In political terms he was the anti-Abbott.

Tony Crook from the far west went completely the other way: his full price was $850 million, to match the share of mining royalties the Western Australian Nats had extorted from their state government to bankroll the bush. But he was totally against any tax on the miners to pay for it. Not overly appealing to Gillard.

And then there was Andrew Wilkie, back in the picture as his Tasmanian seat of Denison belatedly swung away from Labor. Wilkie's aim was 'ethical' government; he himself was so determined to preserve his moral purity that he declined to join the rural three even in the initial stage of meeting the two party leaders. He had absolutely no position, he explained; he could support Labor, or Liberal, or neither. Given his outspoken opposition to the war in Iraq and his previous incarnation as a Green Senate candidate, it was assumed that he at least inclined to the left, but he now claimed to have no ideology whatsoever. He would, however, like legislation to limit poker machines and to protect whistleblowers, and a new hospital would be nice. And there were a few other goodies which he was sure both sides would be happy to provide.

To handle their side of the negotiations, Julia Gillard nominated herself and Wayne Swan, which seemed obvious enough. Tony Abbott opted to be joined by his Liberal deputy, Julie Bishop, and not by the man who would be deputy prime minister in a Coalition government, Warren Truss; for the purposes of the meetings, the Nationals were deemed not to exist. Abbott did his best to prepare the ground. The independents had all been talking about reforming the operations of parliament and working towards a more cooperative and collegiate system; Abbott, who had made his parliamentary reputation as a brutal and ruthless attack dog, now mused of his belief that we could have a 'kinder, gentler polity ...'

226

His newfound tenderness quickly evaporated when the independents presented him with a list which included the demand that both sides submit their policies to the Treasury for costing and comment. Abbott refused point-blank: he wasn't going to tug his forelock to every demand like Julia Gillard did. He would give the Treasury nothing unless and until the police uncovered and charged the source of the leak that had appeared during the campaign. His stance had looked spurious at the time, and now it was downright silly: the election was over, the policies were settled and were supposed to be public, so what did he have to hide? If he became prime minister, all his policies would have to go to Treasury anyway, so why not now? And in any case the police were highly unlikely to uncover the leak; the only leaker in recent history to have suffered that fate was the Liberals' own Godwin Grech, and he had virtually given himself up. Abbott's obstinacy clearly had very little to do with principle and a lot to do with the fear that Treasury would find that the assumptions on which he had based his costings were unrealistic, if not downright deceitful, and blow the lid off whatever economic credibility he had laboriously acquired.

The independents were not impressed; the refusal would, they said, make it difficult for them to support Abbott. Gillard, true to form, agreed to everything, but even she blanched at the boldness of some of the demands. The independents wanted comprehensive briefings from no less than ten ministers and their shadows, and, setting an extraordinary precedent, private audiences with the permanent heads of Treasury and the finance department. They wanted the loan of senior and experienced advisers – Bruce Hawker from the Labor side and Grahame Morris and Arthur Sinodinos (exhumed from the past like Silenus) from the Libs. As well as improvements to the parliamentary process they wanted to discuss changes to the rules

227

surrounding government advertising, political donations and public funding. And as a non-negotiable finale, they insisted on a signed and sealed guarantee that neither leader, having become prime minister, would call an early election; the parliament would run the full term. Just about the only thing they did not ask for was a referendum for fixed four-year terms as adopted by some of the states, and one suspected that the omission would be filled in as soon as they thought of it.

The list was extravagant to the point of being outrageous; even incoming prime ministers did not get to see the Treasury evaluation of their opponents' promises. But there was no indication that the 'three amigos,' as they were now being dubbed in memory of the unlamented Sol Trujillo's gang of enforcers, regarded it as an ambit claim; they were deadly serious. Which was more than could be said of the Liberal response. Having been ridiculed by both the independents and the commentators for his use of the leak as an excuse for non-compliance, Abbott now scrambled for the high ground: to reveal Treasury deliberations to outsiders would not only be an unacceptable breach of the conventions surrounding caretaker government, it would also end the bond of confidentiality between all governments and their closest advisers; public servants would no longer feel able to give the frank and fearless advice on which their political masters relied. Oh, and incidentally, Treasury couldn't really understand Opposition policies anyway; only the Opposition could. Andrew Robb, apparently unaware that his role as campaign spokesman had ended with the campaign itself, assured anyone who would listen that the real issues were paying the debt, ending the waste, stopping the taxes and turning back the boats. The independents declared that Abbott obviously had something to hide and returned to their electorates for the weekend, only to be assailed by Liberal and National supporters telling them to back Abbott or else.

The good news was that the doubtful seats were finally sorting themselves out. Labor hung on to Corangamite and Hasluck went to the Libs, giving the House of Representatives its first indigenous member in Ken Wyatt. The Libs had also given us the first indigenous senator in Neville Bonner, but had then cut off his preselection when the seat was required for someone seen as more important. It was to be hoped that Wyatt would receive better treatment. The seat of Brisbane remained undecided, but was likely to go to the Libs. However you played it, no one could form a government without the support of at least three of the four remaining independents.

There were those who maintained that, in the circumstances, it was hardly worth forming a government at all; one of these was the *Australian*'s Dennis Shanahan, who urged a return to the polls, presumably in the hope that a second round would see his mate Tony Abbott emerge triumphant. The Greens' Bob Brown suggested that this might be the motive behind Abbott's intransigence over the Treasury costings; after all, none of the other explanations made sense. But Barnaby Joyce, providing a rare glimpse of a National in the media, dismissed the idea. No one, he pointed out, wanted to go through that again in the foreseeable future. But perhaps one person did. The preposterous Steve Fielding, the accidental senator from Family First, would, like the rest of the old Senate, retain his seat until 1 July next year. Asked whether he would allow a minority Labor government to pursue its agenda, he temporised; indeed, he did not even rule out blocking supply. Actually, supply for the year had already been passed in the budget session, so Fielding's threat was as ignorant as it was arrogant. But, he warned, it was something the governor-general should

bear in mind if she was looking for stability: he was not convinced that the Labor government deserved a second chance.
That's right, he, him, the man who received just 0.08 per cent
of the first-preference vote in 2004 – just four-fifths of one-
hundredth of one state, about three-fifths of five-eighths of
fuck all in today's money – considered that he had the right to
decide who should govern Australia in 2010. And conservative
commentators were accusing the independents of having ideas
above their station!

In fact the governor-general was unlikely to come into it at
all, except to rubber-stamp whatever happened in parliament.
Some of the sillier commentators had become excited about
how the G-G, Quentin Bryce, was the mother-in-law of Labor
MP Bill Shorten, and conjectured that this would put her in a
conflict of interest when it came to choosing who would be
prime minister. But it would not be her choice. Julia Gillard
remained prime minister, albeit in a caretaker role, until the poll
was declared. As soon as it was, Bryce was bound by convention
to ask her if she could form a government; if she said yes, she
would be commissioned. If she said no, or if she subsequently
lost a vote of confidence in the House of Representatives, Bryce
would offer the job to Tony Abbott. If both leaders failed, she
would have to prorogue parliament and call an election. It was
all quite straightforward, not at all like the deadlock between
the House of Reps and the Senate in 1975. Those who were
trying to make it a new crisis just didn't understand.

At least Tony Abbott finally faced reality; he sent a message
after the departing independents saying he had decided to
submit his costings to Treasury after all and Treasury could tell
the independents about them, so long as the independents
didn't tell Julia Gillard or Wayne Swan. Abbott portrayed this
as a win, but in fact it was an inevitable back-down given the

circumstances. Andrew Robb had already been caught out; Robb had claimed that the Federal Police investigation of the leak was already well under way and a result could be expected any day now. The police replied that there was no investigation; they were still considering whether to open one. But more importantly, opinion was turning against the Opposition. The suspicion was that they were actually trying to set the scene for another election, preferably one which would run early next year, when the hated New South Wales Labor government would also be facing the people. This, it was believed, would make Abbott prime minister in his own right.

It might; but the downside was that the voters would be outraged at being forced back to the polls. They had been through all that, they had delivered their verdict – well, sort of – and it was up to the politicians to make it work. The umpire's decision should be respected and those who tried to ignore it would pay. It was a risk Abbott was not prepared to take, especially when his friends in the media were ramping up the pressure on the independents to give him the guernsey. The News Limited groups produced a series of surveys designed to prove that the voters in all three electorates wanted a Coalition government. Actually they didn't; they wanted their local member to remain independent, which was why they had voted for him. And there was no reason why the independents should not follow this course; they could simply agree not to vote no-confidence and to guarantee supply, and the government could continue as usual. But, following the protocol outlined above, that would leave Labor in power, an outcome utterly unacceptable to the Murdoch press. And in any case it would be naïve to expect the three independents to pass up the once-in-a-lifetime opportunity for power and glory the hung parliament presented; so the horse-trading continued.

It was messy, but it was undeniably intriguing; like a good murder mystery, it made you pay attention right up to the last page. Suddenly politics was interesting and even relevant; the punters genuinely wanted to know what was going on, how many options there were, what were the rules of the game and who was up who for the rent. The *Sydney Morning Herald* produced a four-page wrap-around attempting to explain it; the public learned more about politics in the last week of August than they had in twelve years of high school. Whether the interest could be maintained was, of course, another question; technically the impasse could drag on until the end of November, when parliament would be forced to sit and make a decision. But no one expected it to go on for that long. Back in Canberra, on the last day of winter, it was clear the climax was approaching. Or was it? Would all voters please remain seated and keep your seat belts securely fastened until the election has come to a complete halt ...

> *Come, children, let us shut up the box and*
> *the puppets, for our play is played out.*
> —WILLIAM MAKEPEACE THACKERAY

★ 15.

IT HAD TO BE SAID that most of the passengers were in no real hurry to disembark anyway. Life without a federal government was turning out to be not very different from life with one. Normal services continued to be provided much as they always had been and society remained as functional (or dysfunctional) as it had ever been. This was a seriously alarming state of affairs: if it went on for much longer people would start asking if the Commonwealth parliament was really necessary, from which it would be only a short step to wondering whether the politicians themselves could be made redundant. Mere anarchy would be loosed upon the world. Fortunately the media held the line: while the government and the parliament might be on indefinite pause, the process of politics continued unabated.

Indeed, if anything it moved into entirely new territory. The prospect of minority government was a fascinating one, mainly because of the uncertainties it offered. The general view was that there were only four real independents left in play: the three amigos, Tony Windsor, Rob Oakeshott and Bob Katter, and the Tasmanian, Andrew Wilkie. The Green, Adam Bandt, was more or less committed to Labor and it was impossible to see the West Australian National, Tony Crook, deserting the Coalition; he had already attended a meeting with the other Nationals and was bitterly opposed to a mining tax, which seemed to settle the matter. The Liberal Alby Schultz, who seemed determined to take over Wilson Tuckey's role as the party's resident mad uncle, was vitriolic about Crook, fuming that not only had he stood against a sitting Liberal but – the ultimate crime – he had been elected on Labor preferences. True, but that is how the preferential system works; in any three-cornered contest the preferences have to go somewhere. Schultz might also have reflected that it was Liberal prefer-ences that got both Wilkie and Bandt over the line.

Another contender for Tuckey's crown was Wild Bill Hef-fernan, who rang Rob Oakeshott's home and announced to his bewildered wife that it was the devil calling for her husband. Even more alarmingly, he apologised by saying he thought he had been talking to one of the children. Windsor laughed it off, but Oakeshott was not amused and suggested Tony Abbott was having a problem keeping his fringe dwellers under control. And there were rumblings coming from the body of the National Party, which was seriously miffed at the fact that the amigos – National Party rats – were now being treated with fawning generosity, while the old Nats – the faithful partners of the Libs for so long – were, as usual, being taken for granted. If any favours were being doled out, they wanted to be first in the queue.

It was a healthy reminder that every Coalition government was, in a sense, a minority Liberal Party government; the Libs very seldom had the numbers to govern in their own right, and when they did were unwilling to try it because they knew they would need the Nats again in future. And this time the Nats were in a very strong position: for the first time almost in living memory they had actually increased their numbers, and of course they were needed more than ever. And they had not yet signed a coalition agreement for the next parliamentary term. But the Nats were not a completely cohesive force. There were the old-style Nats from New South Wales and Victoria, now sitting with some (but not all) of the amalgamated Lib-Nats from Queensland, the Country Liberal Party Nats from the Northern Territory, and, for at least part of the time, Tony Crook. If this motley collection held together, it would total seventy-three votes; whatever happened, Abbott would need three of the four independents to form government; and so, of course, would Julia Gillard.

The problem was that as the second week of stalemate got under way, Wilkie looked like a very loose cannon; there was the real prospect that he would remain as a genuine independent, reserving the right to support either side as and when he saw fit. So it came down to the amigos. For either side to gain a clear majority, the three would have to decide and vote as a unit, and they had already said that this was not part of the deal; they would stick together for the purposes of negotiations, but then it was every amigo for himself. The prospect was grim, but obviously it was vital for all the independents that a government – any government – was formed. The only alternative was another election, and while no one was willing to predict which way that would break, it was unlikely that Australia would produce a second hung parliament. The independents' power and influence depended on holding the balance; under normal circumstances they would be simple backbenchers – assuming, of course, that they held their seats; if they were seen to be responsible for another election, the voters could well decide they were more trouble than they were worth.

But if it was in the interests of the independents to avoid a return to the polls, it was even more important to the major parties, who were not only exhausted but flat, stony broke. Their usual donors were unlikely to kick the tin to any worthwhile extent so soon after the last fiasco, and public funding, while generous by any normal standards, would not be enough to finance the sort of desperate campaign that would be required to force an unwilling electorate to deliver the goods. And so the dickering resumed. The amigos went off to their various official briefings with departmental heads, whose reaction to this unprecedented imposition is unfortunately not recorded. Wilkie presented his wish list to both Gillard and Abbott; Gillard replied promptly with what Wilkie described as an 'offer,' which he obviously saw as no more than a basis for further haggling.

Both sides started grasping at straws. The two-party-preferred vote had long been a bone of contention: the Coalition had claimed a win early on election night, then Labor had claimed it back, and now the Coalition was again claiming a majority. It was left to the Electoral Commission to explain that it all depended on how you measured it, and in any case they wouldn't have final figures for weeks. But the real point was that it was entirely irrelevant, as was the primary vote, which Abbott was bragging about. Under the Australian constitution it is the number of seats that count; in the recent past both sides have formed government with less than half the popular vote. That emu would not fly.

Labor's Craig Emerson was more lateral. Labor members, he pointed out, were bound to vote with their party, while Liberals and Nationals weren't; they could and did cross the floor occasionally. This had always been held up as a conservative commitment to freedom and individuality, a positive virtue.

But in the present circumstances it was a recipe for chaos; a couple of Libs exercising their conscience over something like the reintroduction of temporary protection visas for refugees could derail the whole show. The Labor system might be authoritarian, but it was the only one that could guarantee stability, and that was what everyone said they cared about. And then there was the Senate: only Labor could work with the Greens to deliver predictable outcomes. Why, there was even talk of a formal coalition ...

It appeared that Labor was taking the initiative, and Abbott felt the need to call a very gung-ho joint party meeting to respond. He oozed confidence and bravado: the Coalition, he said, was now 'a government in waiting.' Well, maybe, but Labor was still the government in office, albeit in caretaker mode, and Gillard took full advantage of the status to address the National Press Club as prime minister. She had nothing much to say, but the fact that she was there to say it was probably a plus. The most salient point was a commitment to parliamentary reform, which Oakeshott in particular saw as a necessary step from both sides before proceeding to final talks. Gillard seemed open to the idea of a more civilised and inclusive way of doing business, but there came a point at which, uncharacteristically, she drew the line: Bob Katter's desire for a return to tariff protection was quite simply not on. Was Gillard going to turn out to be a tough negotiator after all?

No, actually. The next big announcement was that she had signed an agreement with the Greens: in return for the support of Adam Bandt (which had already been tacitly guaranteed), he and Bob Brown would be given weekly access to her office and would be briefed and consulted on all impending legislation. It was a privilege available to very few government backbenchers and not even to all ministers; it wasn't actually coalition (Brown had not been offered a ministry) but it was a very close form of alliance. As well as admission to the inner circle, Brown got agreement to a list of policy commitments. Most related to process: reform of political funding, legislation for truth in political advertising, a debates commission, a parliamentary budget committee, a parliamentary integrity commissioner, prompt release of parliamentary documents, more time for private member's bills and a move towards fixed three-year terms (why not four? Oh, New South Wales). But there were a few ideas with wider implications: a referendum to recognise indigenous Australians in the constitution and another to do the same for local government; a full parliamentary debate about Afghanistan; and the formation of a joint climate-change committee to consider the best and quickest way of putting a price on carbon.

This last would pre-empt Gillard's much-derided citizens' assembly, although she still bravely insisted that could take place later, and also provided Abbott with his best line for a new scare campaign – or rather, an old one: price on carbon equals great big new tax on everything. The alliance also put a big dent in Labor's conservative credentials, which it was using to woo the three rural independents. The Greens might be gradually shedding their reputation as a party of feral tree-huggers dedicated to vegetarianism, abortion and sodomy, but they were proudly and undeniably a progressive party, well to the left of modern Labor. A formal partnership with them was a risk; and what did Labor get in return? Support that had already been promised and, in any case, was heavily qualified: Bandt reserved his right to vote against any bills except those regarding supply and motions of no confidence. But the same promise applied if a Coalition government under Tony Abbott was formed. The only real benefit for Labor was psychological.

Given that Tony Crook had announced that he was dissatisfied with Abbott's bid for his support and would definitely sit on the crossbenches, the numbers were now technically Labor 73, Coalition 72. But given that Crook was never going to vote Labor into government, in practical terms they remained 73-all. No progress to report.

But then, next morning, came what should have been the circuit-breaker: the independents released the Treasury review of the costing of election promises. Labor's were pretty much on track; they were even a hundred million or so in the black. But the Coalition was out by anywhere between $7 billion – that's seven thousand million – and $10.6 billion, a miscalculation so horrendous that it was immediately dubbed a black hole. Julia Gillard and Wayne Swan crowed that this showed why Abbott had refused to comply with the charter of budget honesty before the election: he had indeed had something to hide – about 10 billion somethings, in fact. His claims to economic management and responsibility now lay in tatters. Abbott admitted somewhat sheepishly that there had indeed been discussions about the costings: Shadow Treasurer Joe Hockey called it a difference of opinion. But the hard fact was that Treasury had a lot more experience and resources to make the calculations than Abbott and Hockey. In any test of credibility, it was no contest. If the blunder had been revealed before the election, it would almost certainly have blown Abbott out of the race. But now the judges were not an amorphous mass of voters but four heavily self-interested politicians. They all said that the news would have an impact on their deliberations, but none suggested that it would be decisive.

On the very same day, it was clear that in at least one case it had not been. Andrew Wilkie called a press conference to announce that he too had signed an agreement with Gillard to

be her new best friend. As in the case of Bandt, Wilkie's agreement amounted to little more than that: he too would consider
all bills on their merits and would not support blocking supply
or frivolous no-confidence motions – against whomever was
prime minister. And like Bandt, Wilkie got a lot in return for
very little: the promise of restrictions on poker machines, with
the threat of legislation if necessary, and the release of a lot
more money for hospitals, with special attention to his own
hospital in Hobart. Abbott was seriously annoyed. He had
feigned indignation with Bandt for not negotiating with the
Coalition – although he must have known that they didn't have
a lot to talk about – but he had considered himself a real chance
with Wilkie. And he had bid real money: in response to Wilkie's
passionate pleas for the Hobart hospital, Abbott had put a cool
billion on the table, hard cash, small unmarked notes delivered
on the spot. Now Wilkie had knocked it back for about a third
of the amount. Not only that, but he had called the offer irresponsible, particularly in view of the black hole in the election
costings. Didn't he know that under the Coalition, surpluses
would always be bigger and interest rates lower and sex would
last longer – no, scratch that. But everyone knows, life's better
under the conservatives.

As with the signing of Bandt, the significance of Wilkie's
arrival in the tent was largely symbolic, but it did provide
momentum. Labor was now indisputably ahead on the seats,
74–73. Three remained to count. As sporting commentators
like to put it, there were three possible results: Labor could win
or the Coalition could win or it could be a tie. Wilkie said he
hoped his decision would push the amigos towards making a
unanimous decision for Labor; that would give the new government the buffer of a spare seat and would greatly improve the
chance of a stable three years. But he admitted he really had no

idea. One widely held view was that Rob Oakeshott was leaning towards Labor, but Tony Windsor and Bob Katter would go the other way, thus producing the dreaded tie and a return to the polls – unless, as was rumoured, Labor was able to entice a renegade moderate from the Coalition side with the offer of the speakership. Katter said he was making his mind up every quarter of an hour, which didn't help. He had been spotted dining with Kevin Rudd, which further confused the issue: the Labor people could not decide whether this was a matter for celebration or despair. But the public mood was becoming clearer. It had been fun, but enough was enough. Three of the original six were now locked in. As the second week of political limbo drew to an end, it was time for the amigos to make up their minds, cast their lot, bite the bullet and take the plunge.

Windsor went home to Tamworth for a final rumination; Oakeshott remained in Canberra to conclude his negotiations for parliamentary reform with Labor's Anthony Albanese and the Liberals' Christopher Pyne – once again the Nationals were non-participants. Katter stayed in the capital as well and supped with the Devil (Bill Heffernan). He insisted that nothing should be read into this; after all, he also supped with Kevin Rudd. He had yet another non-negotiable demand: the end of the duopoly between Coles and Woolworths. But this tended to be swamped by last-minute pleas from the conservative side, which were becoming seriously desperate and quite shrill. Scott Morrison, for instance, was all but hysterical: the independents could not go to Labor, he shrieked, because Labor wouldn't stop the boats! Andrew Robb was even more apocalyptic, warning that the Green–Labor (in that order) alliance would produce the most left-wing government in Australia's history, even more extreme than that of Gough Whitlam. Yes, that would be the mad Whitlam government that introduced Medibank and free tertiary education. Perhaps not the best comparison to draw at that moment.

Then the weekend papers brought in the really bad news: both the Fairfax press and the *Australian* had done their polling, and both found a majority of voters in favour of the independents joining Julia Gillard to form a Labor government. The *Australian* ran the story as just two paragraphs low down on the front page, emphasising that this was not what the independents' own constituents wanted – yes, but the poll that showed them favouring the Coalition was done before the revelations about Tony Abbott's $10-billion costings error, characterised by the paper's economic apologist Michael Stutchbury as 'not a black hole – just a couple of potholes, really.' Some potholes. Just to make it clear what it thought was really important, the national daily ran the screaming headline: 'Greens to rush same-sex bill.' It was a fitting note on which to end its election coverage: self-seeking, trivial, misleading and very, very dumb. Tony Abbott interrupted everyone's day of rest by using the Sunday press for an appeal to the independents which wavered between the plaintive and the threatening. And Galaxy had yet another poll on Monday which found that more than half the voters would actually prefer another election to minority government by either side. At which point the three amigos reassembled at Parliament House to bring, we all hoped, at least a semblance of order out of the political chaos.

Naturally they received plenty of last-minute advice. Noel Pearson begged Rob Oakeshott, who has an Aboriginal-Islander wife, to support Tony Abbott, partly because he saw Abbott as a friend, but mainly because he hated the Greens. The veteran independent Ted Mack said the three should all go to Labor because that would give their electorates the best deal: obviously the Nats, who wanted to reclaim the seats, would play a spoiling role if they supported the Coalition. The Libs' Warren Entsch, who had won back the electorate next door to Bob Katter's, urged his neighbour to stop playing to the gallery and get on with making a decision; Katter responded with a bravura but thoroughly confusing performance on *Q&A*. Windsor said he was leaning towards one side but wouldn't even tell his wife which. They seemed determined to milk the last dregs of drama from their temporary role as kingmakers.

But they did find time to clear up the loose ends: they signed an agreement on parliamentary reform with Albanese and Pyne, afterwards indulging in a group hug which was about as convincing as the ritual handshakes between the Israeli and Palestinian leaders at the opening of yet another doomed round of peace talks. With any luck the Australian pact would be a lit-tle more successful, but in spite of the ritual expressions of good intentions it was never going to herald a utopian era of peace, love and brown rice. Australian politics is intrinsically antago-nistic – a contest between competing interests for the advan-tage of one over the other. Oakeshott might fantasise about cooperation and harmony, but it wasn't going to happen. The parties had been known to declare a temporary truce at times of national emergency (and to the parties a hung parliament was just such a time), but it never lasted. The likelihood was that once things got back to normal, whichever side gained the incumbency would go back to abusing the process to the maxi-mum possible extent. Anyone who doubted this truism need only look at the New South Wales parliament, which had gone through the same exercise of independent-driven reform as recently as 1991. Fewer than twenty years later it was once again a by-word for sleaze, scandal and brutality. The only bit of reform that had survived was the fixed four-year term, and a lot of people wished it hadn't.

Still, the three amigos had their moment of triumph, which was all that mattered on the day. They also persuaded Tony Crook to declare his support for the Coalition – sort of; he was even less explicit than Andrew Wilkie had been when he went through the same ritual for Labor, but it enabled the three hold-outs to declare that the numbers were now such that both sides could, in theory at least, reach the magical figure of seventy-six. They, and they alone, would determine which. The popular view was that they would favour Labor; the media were full of stories about how Gillard had the momentum and the tacticians on the Liberal side were deeply pessimistic. Even the redoubtable Barnaby Joyce seemed ready to throw in the towel. That the independents would deliver government to Labor was seen almost as a *fait accompli*.

Frankly I doubted it. From the first my instinct had been that they would eventually come down on the side of the conservatives and nothing much had happened to change that. The fact that the popular view was to the contrary merely confirmed my opinion: the independents were the kind of perverse types who would go against the popular view just for the hell of it. The only hope for Labor was that the independents would not want to be seen to be doing the bidding of the Murdoch press. But then, whatever they did would please some of their enemies and infuriate some of their friends. Perhaps being a kingmaker wasn't going to be quite as much fun as it had seemed during the heady days of the interregnum. They locked themselves into Windsor's office for the final countdown. The press conference was scheduled for three o'clock, then moved forward to two – the thought was perhaps they had reached an early, unanimous decision. Then it was put back to three. And then Bob Katter, playing the drama queen to the last, burst into the room and said that he had made up his mind and he wasn't going to wait for the others: he was going with Tony Abbott, who had offered him eight items out of his wish list of twenty, while Gillard had offered only one. But if his old mate Kevin Rudd had still been leading Labor, he would have gone with Kevin.

Katter made the numbers 74-all. Windsor and Oakeshott were left holding the keys to the kingdom. The immediate thinking was that they would probably go to Gillard; if they were going with Abbott there was no need for Katter to have held his separate press conference. But of course they could still split and deliver us back to the polls, a thought almost too terrible to contemplate. They didn't. Shortly after three, Windsor, relaxed and even jovial, arrived and explained clearly and concisely why he had chosen Labor. Broadband and climate change were important, as were the new opportunities for rural Australia; but the key was stability. As he pointed out later, he didn't trust Abbott not to rush to an election as soon as the opportunity arose, while it would clearly be in Gillard's interest to hang in there. And then Oakeshott rose and waffled on for twenty minutes about what had gone on in his cluttered mind, but no one was really listening. Windsor's decision meant that Abbott could not form a government; even if Oakeshott went with him, he would still be stuck on seventy-five. The glorious future Oakeshott was describing could only exist if he stuck with Windsor and gave Gillard the magic seventy-six, which he finally got around to confirming in what had become a stunning anti-climax. And so it was left to Julia Eileen Gillard to declare herself, at last, ready to move into the Lodge.

The timing could hardly have been better: 7 September was an auspicious day for red-headed sheilas. The most celebrated of them all, Elizabeth I, England's Gloriana, had been born on that date just 477 years earlier. She too had had the odd run-in with a Mad Monk or two, but was generally thought to have done pretty well. Of course, the omens were not all favourable: exactly seventy-four years ago the last thylacine died, making extinct a unique Australian. There had been times in 2010 when it looked as if Australian democracy might suffer the same fate. Somehow it had been given a second chance, and while its future was unlikely to be quite as bright as Rob Oakeshott was forecasting, the parliament was preparing to boldly go where no Australian parliament had ever ventured before. At the very least, the challenge would be intriguing. Let the games begin.